*More than Christians* jolted me wit[h] eloquently reminds his readers tha[t] true, our words have power, and the language of the Bible is beautiful. Now, maybe more than ever, Christian language needs to be infused with biblical wording that accurately reflects the heart of God for all people.

**KAT ARMSTRONG,** author of the Storyline Bible Studies series and host of the *Holy Curiosity* podcast

Norman Hubbard has been a like a brother to me for years, but it wasn't until I read his brilliant book about gospel-shaped community and language that I understood why. Accessible, sharp, and biblically wise, this is New Testament theology at its best, the kind of work that illuminates your mind, reprioritizes your relationships, and engages you with Jesus and his gospel again as if for the first time.

**TRENT SHEPPARD,** author of *Jesus Journey* and director of training at Youth with a Mission's University of the Nations in Kona, Hawaii

In *More than Christians: Practicing Gospel-Shaped Community with the Language of the Early Church,* author Norman Hubbard guides readers in an accessible exploration of the labels New Testament writers used to describe Christ followers. In Hubbard's hands common labels get explored, adjusted, and restored as he tells us who we are. *More than Christians* deserves to be savored, underlined, considered, weighed, and applied in community.

**SANDRA L. GLAHN,** professor of media arts and worship at Dallas Theological Seminary

Have you ever read a work on something that you thought you had considered thoroughly only to feel like you hadn't even started? Hubbard has created that experience here in *More than Christians*. I have taught lessons to my students about the revolutionary way the early Christians saw and referenced each other. However, this book challenged me to look again and consider whether there is more to this than I had realized. It challenged me to make practical changes and be more intentional with the words that I use to talk about fellow believers. It might just be that those changes are key to changing a Christian culture looking to find its way again.

**MARTY SOLOMON,** creator of *The BEMA Podcast* and author of *Asking Better Questions of the Bible*

A timeless gem especially relevant for us today. We desperately need to understand and reclaim the power of how early believers addressed one another. As Norman Hubbard beautifully writes, these words—*brothers* and *sisters, beloved, saints, disciples, fellow workers,* and *Christians*—powerfully proclaim the gospel, our identity in Christ, and our relationship to one another. Jews and Gentiles now belong to the same family and call each other brothers and sisters. Former enemies are now beloved because we are first loved by God. When we surrender our lives to Christ, we become saints, disciples, and fellow workers in the Kingdom, striving toward a common goal. By using these names, we can shape how we see and treat one another, bringing reconciliation, purpose, and unity to our communities today.

**JOYCE KOO DALRYMPLE,** founder and CEO of Refuge for Strength women's ministry, Bible study author, and podcast host

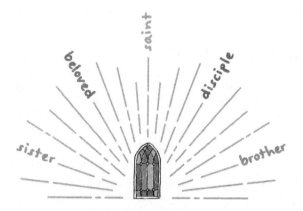

beloved · saint · disciple · sister · brother

# MORE THAN CHRISTIANS

Practicing Gospel-Shaped Community
with the Language of the
Early Church

## NORMAN HUBBARD

NavPress

A NavPress resource published in alliance
with Tyndale House Publishers

NavPress.com

*More than Christians: Practicing Gospel-Shaped Community with the Language of the Early Church*

Copyright © 2025 by Norman Hubbard. All rights reserved.

A NavPress resource published in alliance with Tyndale House Publishers

*NavPress* and the NavPress logo are registered trademarks of NavPress, The Navigators, Colorado Springs, CO. *Tyndale* is a registered trademark of Tyndale House Ministries. Absence of ® in connection with marks of NavPress or other parties does not indicate an absence of registration of those marks.

The Team:
David Zimmerman, Publisher; Olivia Eldredge, Developmental Editor; Elizabeth Schroll, Copyeditor; Ron C. Kaufmann, Designer; Sarah K. Johnson, Proofreading Coordinator

Cover and interior illustration of Gothic window copyright © by Corna_L/Depositphotos. All rights reserved. Cover and interior illustration of sunrays copyright © by Alena Melicharkova/ Depositphotos. All rights reserved.

Author photo copyright © 2024 by Chris Kuhlow. All rights reserved.

Unless otherwise indicated, all Scripture quotations are taken from the (NASB®) New American Standard Bible,® copyright © 1960, 1962, 1963, 1968, 1971, 1972, 1973, 1975, 1977, 1995 by The Lockman Foundation. Used by permission. All rights reserved. www.lockman.org. Scripture quotations marked ESV are from The ESV® Bible (The Holy Bible, English Standard Version®), copyright © 2001 by Crossway, a publishing ministry of Good News Publishers. Used by permission. All rights reserved. Scripture quotations marked MSG are taken from *The Message*, copyright © 1993, 2002, 2018 by Eugene H. Peterson. Used by permission of NavPress. All rights reserved. Represented by Tyndale House Publishers. Scripture quotations marked NEB are taken from *The New English Bible*, copyright © 1970, Oxford University Press, Cambridge University Press. Scripture quotations marked NET are taken from the New English Translation, NET Bible,® copyright © 1996–2006 by Biblical Studies Press, L.L.C. http://netbible.com. All rights reserved. Scripture quotations marked NIV are taken from the Holy Bible, *New International Version*,® NIV.® Copyright © 1973, 1978, 1984, 2011 by Biblica, Inc.® Used by permission. All rights reserved worldwide.

In Scripture quotations, all italics have been added by the author for emphasis.

Some of the anecdotal illustrations in this book are true to life and are included with the permission of the persons involved. All other illustrations are composites of real situations, and any resemblance to people living or dead is purely coincidental.

For information about special discounts for bulk purchases, please contact Tyndale House Publishers at csresponse@tyndale.com, or call 1-855-277-9400.

ISBN 978-1-64158-696-2

Printed in the United States of America

| 31 | 30 | 29 | 28 | 27 | 26 | 25 |
|----|----|----|----|----|----|----|
| 7  | 6  | 5  | 4  | 3  | 2  | 1  |

*In loving memory of my late wife,*

*Katie Hubbard*

*(December 17, 1971–January 25, 2016)*

*This book is dedicated to*
*Charles and Betsy Hansen.*
*You persisted in calling me "Son" until I was able*
*to call you "Mom and Dad."*

# Contents

*The disciples were first called Christians in Antioch.*

ACTS 11:26

Introduction

# THE GOSPEL AND THE GAPS
# THAT SEPARATE US

The gospel is "the power of God for salvation" (Romans 1:16). Most Christians believe this with all their hearts, but more than a few of us assume it *only* means "Jesus has saved my soul." What if the gospel means more than profound personal transformation? What if the Cross also changes your relationships? In other words, what might it mean for the gospel to answer two questions: not just *Who am* I *in Christ?* but also *Who are we in Christ?*

The gospel does not simply save your soul by changing your relationship with God. It also transforms your community by changing your relationships with everyone who believes in Jesus.

I probably don't need to point this out to you, but our communities are getting more fragmented as we grow more diverse. Ironically enough, the closer we get, the more separate we become. And, shockingly, the tribalism that defines our life in the world doesn't look much different inside a church. We have painted ourselves into Christian enclaves that make the New Testament gospel look like a work of fiction. We are modeling a gospel that says God can change a human heart but not a human network. That is not a whole gospel.

The early church believed, as we do, that the gospel was "the power of God for salvation to everyone who believes, to the Jew first and also to the Greek" (Romans 1:16). They knew the gospel did more than transform individual hearts, ideas, or privately held convictions. They knew their relationships with one another had also been reconfigured at the Cross.[1]

When God saves us, he places us in a new family, among a new people. The evidence of new life within us reveals itself in the kinds of relationships we build precisely because God has brought a new kind of human community into existence. This book will focus on such reconfigured relationships by paying particular attention to the words we use *to identify and build up this community.*

As a starting point in this exploration, we observe what Luke affirms in Acts 11:26: There was a time when Christians didn't call each other "Christians." In fact, no one seems to have used the term *Christian* for the first fifteen years of the church's history. At least, the evidence (or silence!) of Scripture seems to indicate this. It also seems clear enough that the earliest Christians never called *each other* "Christians" at all. Calling someone a "Christian" was originally a *non-Christian* thing to do. There's a good chance the term was a put-down, not a neutral label.

Apart from Luke's mention in Acts 11:26, there are only two other times when the word *Christian* (Greek *Christianos*) is used in the Bible, and *both* imply that being called a "Christian" was not exactly a compliment:

- "Agrippa replied to Paul, 'In a short time you will persuade me to become *a Christian*'" (Acts 26:28).

- "Make sure that none of you suffers as a murderer, or thief, or evildoer, or a troublesome meddler; but if anyone suffers *as a Christian*, he is not to be ashamed, but is to glorify God in this name" (1 Peter 4:15-16).

People who think of the word *Christian* positively today tend to misread these passages. In Acts 26:28, Agrippa appears to be rebuffing Paul's bold witness by saying something like "Surely you don't think you could convince me to join this questionable sect of 'Christians' so effortlessly, right?" The context of 1 Peter 4:15-16 is also very clear. Calling someone a "Christian" was tantamount to an accusation, like calling them a murderer.[2] In short, it was not a compliment.

So if Christians didn't call themselves "Christians" in the New Testament era, what did they call each other? And what does this say about the gospel they had embraced and the community they were forming? These are the primary questions that will guide us as we look at the way Christians talked *to* and *about* one another when the church was just getting off the ground.

These were incomparable years of growth in the church that saw the Christian movement transformed from a marginal Jewish sect in Judea into a multinational phenomenon spread across the Roman Empire. The rise of Christianity baffled the leaders of the day, and it still baffles people today. The Christian movement should have been another footnote in history, like the Bar Kokhba Revolt. (If you don't know much about the Bar Kokhba Revolt, my point is made.) Christianity, however, did not become a footnote but rather a force in human history. Why? How did this happen when there were so many factors working against it? The answer goes beyond the inner transformation of individuals. Becoming a follower of Christ was indeed life-changing, but it was also community transforming. People with only hostility or indifference toward one another experienced a salvation so radical that the polarity of their relationships was reversed, against their expectations. The improbability of this happening cannot be overstated. The cumulative effect of it turned the ancient world upside down.

Today, it's easy to take the meteoric rise of Christianity for granted. It's worth remembering, however, how unlikely it was for Christianity to even get off the starting blocks. After all, the charismatic founder of the movement, Jesus, died roughly three years after beginning it. None of his core group of devotees was remarkable. In fact, they were all Jews, whose fidelity to God and survival in the ancient world often depended on maintaining a sharp separation from the people around them. Building fraternal relationships with Gentiles was not an ideal they gravitated toward.

The Jewish homeland, Judea, was a backwater in the Roman Empire, and the movement itself started in the backwater of that backwater (i.e., Galilee). The followers of Jesus never had political power, nor did they gain any for about three hundred years. The early Christians could not force anyone into their movement. They relied on the persuasiveness of their lives and message alone. There was very little structured leadership in the movement when it began. There were no mysterious rites of initiation, no food laws that set them apart, no unique rituals surrounding childbirth or death, no holy days that everyone observed, and no barriers to whom you could marry (except that a spouse should also be a Christian; see 1 Corinthians 7:39). Pretty much anyone could join the movement, no matter their ethnic background or social status.

So slaves and masters, men and women, Jews and Gentiles all piled into assemblies that should never have gained traction in the first place. They were not told to shave their heads, recite fixed prayers, or walk backward on Thursdays. They didn't kneel in the same direction at the same time of day or make pilgrimages to shrines. In fact, they had no temples, no idols, no sacrifices, no priestly class, and no rituals to speak of beyond baptism (which wasn't unique to them)[3] and bread and wine at communal meals. They were encouraged to live quiet lives within their communities. They were instructed to be virtuous, but that was hardly unique. So how did they grow? How did the early churches establish a social identity clear enough to be noticed, resilient enough to survive, and attractive enough to be desirable? If it wasn't by unique rituals, rigorous rules, rigid hierarchies, or defined institutions, how did they do it?

In short, the early disciples offered something the world desperately needed and couldn't find anywhere else. Folks who study religious movements insist that adherents don't join a new religion if it looks like all the other social groups that have been in town for years. Something must set it apart, something the community hasn't seen before and something people want badly enough to endure the stigma of conversion. So what set the early Christian communities apart? What did their families, masters, neighbors, coworkers, and even antagonists observe? They could not see the Christians' unseen God or their resurrected Savior seated on a heavenly throne, but they could *see* the "intense community" Christians shared and *hear* what they called each other.[4]

British scholar John Barclay insists that "[it was through] the continual affirmation of distinctive Christian identity, a discourse of difference" that the Christian movement was set apart from the world around it.[5] Believers talked like they were a new kind of people and lived like it too. They relied on the power of their words—really, the power of God's Word—to shape a new kind of culture. You could call it a miracle, I suppose, because it was a total miracle that a generation of devout Jews began to call Gentiles their "brothers and sisters." The same could be said of Ananias, the day he met the guy sent to destroy him.

## MEETING YOUR WOULD-BE ASSASSIN FACE-TO-FACE

Saul of Tarsus, whom history knows as the apostle Paul, came into early adulthood with extensive religious training and thorough convictions about proper worship. He was a devout Jew, "devout" with what we would call fanatical zeal. Today's press would likely label him a "violent religious extremist." Paul would probably not disagree, since late in his life he testified to that himself:

> "I lived as a Pharisee according to the strictest sect of our religion. . . .
>
> ". . . I thought to myself that I had to do many things hostile to the name of Jesus of Nazareth. And this is just what I did in Jerusalem; not only did I lock up many of the saints in prisons, having received authority from the chief priests, but also when they were being put to death I cast my vote against them. And as I punished them often in all the synagogues, I tried to force them to blaspheme; and being furiously enraged at them, I kept pursuing them even to foreign cities."
>
> ACTS 26:5, 9-11

Paul didn't just disapprove of Christians. He had marching orders from the religious leaders in Jerusalem to ferret out followers of Jesus "even [in] foreign cities" (Acts 26:11) and force them to renounce their faith.

It was on one such mission that Saul met Jesus face-to-face and lived to tell the tale. The risen Jesus appeared to him personally, led the fanatic to saving faith, and commissioned him to take the gospel to the Gentile world (see Acts 26:12-18). Saul had one small problem, however: Jesus had blinded him in the encounter. Saul had to be led to the house of a man named Judas on Straight Street in Damascus. Presumably, Saul was staying there with the fellow extremists who had accompanied him to the city. We cannot be sure. All we know is that Saul's companions on the Damascus road had heard the sound he'd heard but not encountered the speaker. If Saul had explained any of it to them, there is a good chance they were avoiding him. Had the chief persecutor suddenly converted to the faith he had been persecuting?

Three days after the Damascus-road experience, a man came to the house on Straight Street and asked to see the blinded Saul. The man's name was Ananias, and he was a disciple of Jesus (Acts 9:10). It does not take much imagination to suppose that Ananias was on Saul's list of suspects, and we have every reason to believe that Ananias would have been trying to avoid Saul right up until the moment the Lord appeared to him and told him to go find the fanatic: "Lord, I have heard from many about this man," Ananias replied, "how much harm he did to Your saints at Jerusalem; and here he has authority from the chief priests to bind all who call on Your name" (Acts 9:13-14).

Even so, Ananias obeyed the Lord and went to the house where the extremist sat, blind and praying. Biblical narratives like this draw us into their drama. They invite speculation. We should not build doctrines or denominations on these speculations, but we should be drawn into the drama, asking ourselves, *What if I had been Ananias? How would I have felt walking up to that house on Straight Street?*

For my part, I would have been hoping with all my might that Saul was at the doctor that day. ("Oh, the fanatic isn't in? I'll come back tomorrow.") I would have been running contingency plans in my mind in case things went south. I would have taken some comfort in the fact that, at the very least, the man could not chase me.

There is, of course, no way to know what Ananias was thinking. He was probably not as cynical or cowardly as I am. (But he might have been.) All we know is what Scripture has recorded in the book of Acts. Ananias came into the house, approached the extremist, laid his hands on him, and spoke the first words that Saul heard as a Christian from the lips of another Christian: "*Brother* Saul . . . " (Acts 9:17). This was the first sermon Saul heard as a believer, the gospel in a word.[6] The world has never been the same.

## THE GOSPEL IN A WORD

On his way to Damascus, Saul discovered that Jesus' death had reconciled him to God; in Damascus, Saul discovered that Jesus' death had reconciled him to Ananias, his former enemy. This was the radical restructuring of relationships that defied explanation in the ancient world, yet the earliest generation of Christians knew how to explain it in just a few syllables.

The way early Christians addressed one another—what New Testament professor Paul Trebilco has called the language of "self-designation"[7]—offers us profound insight into the "identity, self-understanding, and character"[8] of the early church. Each time they used words like *sisters* and *brothers* and *saints* and *disciples* to describe their community, they were proclaiming the gospel in a word, identifying themselves as a people in relation to God, to one another, and to the world around.

For the most part, the early church did not invent the words they used. They simply used common words in ways no one else did . . . or could. Christians had a rich register of belonging that shaped a new community amid a worn-out world.

Then, somewhere along the way, we started to call one another "Christians"—just "Christians." Most of us don't mean much by this term anymore. In fact, if we need to make it especially meaningful, we have to add an amplifying adjective and say "Pablo is a *real* Christian." When a noun has to be resuscitated by the adjective *real*, it's time to conduct a postmortem. A word losing its meaning is like a body losing its soul.

The good news is that Jesus Christ knows a thing or two about resurrection. Maybe he can even raise the word *Christian* from the dead in our day. You will have to see for yourself when you reach the final chapter of this book. To get there, I hope you will read the chapters that intervene. Here is what you will discover if you do:

- Chapters 1–3 lay the groundwork for seeing words like *brother* and *beloved* as one-word proclamations of the gospel.

- Chapters 4–5 focus on the phrase *brothers and sisters*, since this is the most prevalent term of self-description in the New Testament. We discover that Christians used this common Jewish term in the most uncommon way possible.

- Chapters 6–10 explore other terms of self-designation adopted by the earliest generation of believers, simple words that formed a gospel-shaped community.

Every term we will study in this book is simple, no more than a few syllables in length. Ordinary people used them in extraordinary ways in the first centuries of the church, and they changed the world as we know it. If we will follow their example, our own communities can't help but be changed. Heaven knows, our worn-out world needs to know today what we called each other when our faith was young.

# 1

# THE POWER OF GOD
# AND THE POWER OF WORDS

God creates new realities and invites his redeemed people to
walk in them. God works in ways only he is capable of, then
asks us to continue working, walking, and talking with him
(and others) to give proper shape to the world he desires.
Understanding God's divine preference for collaboration
is key to understanding the gospel. Sometimes God wants
us to work with our hands. At other times, we're meant to
work with our words. It's important to stress this latter point
because some people assume words simply describe things.
This isn't precisely true: We don't just *say* things with our
words; we *do* things with them. We can't do all the things that
God can do with his words, like making a cosmos, but we do

work with our words, just like we work with our hands. It's part of our endowment from the Creator, one of the many ways he made us with power like his (in kind if not degree). When God creates new realities that we get to walk in, it will almost always involve new patterns of speaking. We see this in the earliest chapters of the Bible, so that is where we will begin.

## GOD'S WORK AND OURS WHEN THE WORLD WAS YOUNG

When God created the world, he spoke it into being. Humans had no part in it since they weren't exactly on the scene to help. On day one of Creation, God simply said, "'Let there be light'; and there was light" (Genesis 1:3). Later, he said things like "'Let the waters below the heavens be gathered into one place, and let the dry land appear'; and it was so" (Genesis 1:9). The repetition of similar refrains throughout the first chapter of Genesis cannot be missed. You get the distinct impression that God can "[call] into being that which does not exist" (Romans 4:17). Unless you stop paying attention to the page in front of you, it cannot "[escape your] notice that *by the word of God* the heavens existed long ago and the earth was formed out of water and by water" (2 Peter 3:5).

What is more, if you believe that Genesis 2 complements the Creation account of Genesis 1, you are left with the distinct impression that the creative work God did during the first week of Creation didn't end on the seventh day when he rested (see Genesis 2:2). He ceased from his labors, but there was more work to do in the weeks—and millennia—ahead. Genesis 2 makes it clear that God's plan was to create a world *and commit its ongoing work into human hands.* At first, "The LORD God took the man [alone] and put him into the garden of Eden to cultivate it and keep it" (Genesis 2:15). We don't know whether Adam thought the work would be difficult. I suppose the notion of begetting children and pruning all those trees by himself would have seemed problematic at best. Adam gets put to work right away, however: "Out of the ground the LORD God formed every beast of the field and every bird of the sky, and brought them to the man *to see what he would call them*; and whatever the man called a living creature, that was its name" (Genesis 2:19). Note that Adam's first task in collaboration with God involves naming things. Saying what something should be called wasn't what Adam did *before* he began to work in the Garden; it *was* his work.

After Adam's first day of work, God drew him into a deep sleep. Then he drew out one of Adam's ribs. Basically, while Adam slept, God kept working. "The LORD God fashioned into a woman the rib which He had taken from the man" (Genesis 2:22). Borrowing a line from Genesis 1, we could say, "And there was evening and there was . . . Eve!" Adam is understandably elated when this happens, and the author of Genesis tells us that he announced, "This is now bone of my bones, / And flesh of my flesh; / *She shall be called Woman,* / Because she was taken out of Man" (Genesis 2:23). I'm not sure whether to call this "word work" or "wordplay" since *woman* and *man* sound alike in Hebrew.[1] The writer then goes on to say that "the man and his wife were both naked and were not ashamed" (Genesis 2:25). This comment builds suspense, since everyone in the audience knows two adults cannot be naked and unashamed for very long.

Genesis 3 tells how quickly the original couple fell into sin and shame. Without being overly simplistic about an epochal text, I want you to note what happens to collaboration and word work in Genesis 3. First, notice that Adam and Eve were not misled by a regular serpent. They were misled by a *talking* serpent. We are not supposed to imagine that, at this point in history, the world was filled with all kinds of talking animals. If they all talked, they would have *introduced themselves* to Adam in Genesis 2. Animals don't talk, at least not in the way that God and humans do. That's why Genesis 3:1 is shocking. Another creature whom God made lower than humans walked up to the woman and began questioning God. One wishes Eve had been a little more taken aback and hit it with a hoe. Instead, she replied. Satan parried her reply by calling God's motives into question. Basically, Satan used his words to twist God's words and Eve's thinking. He didn't force her or Adam to disobey God; he tempted them. This is word work that unmakes a world. What is more, Satan and sin brought division where before there had been unity between God, the man, and the woman. The collaboration that could have marked our world for ages to come turned into a short-lived exercise in innocence that led to ages of shame and blame. If the first two chapters of Genesis had been extended, we could envision a world where heaven and earth cooperated to such an extent that you couldn't tell the two apart. Alas, for that world. It ended in Genesis 3, though we may yet experience it someday.

For now, we inhabit a Genesis 3 world, where Satan uses his words to tempt us and we use ours to wound each other. We self-protect and self-promote rather than working together with our hands and tongues to bring to fruition the world God designed for our blessing. We were put here to shape human culture and harness the power of creation for good. Now we have weeds and weariness, misplaced hopes and miserable victories that dog us to death.

Most people do not even realize there's more to the story than Genesis 3, so dark has this world become. Most don't see the hint dropped at the end of the chapter, where God deliberates within himself—for the third time in three chapters!—about what to do next. Rather than cast humans *from his presence*, God only casts Adam and Eve *from the Garden*: "The LORD God sent [Adam] out from the garden of Eden, to cultivate the ground from which he was taken" (Genesis 3:23). Adam and Eve are sent east of Eden to do *the very same work* they had been commissioned by God to do in Eden. What is more, God remains present to Eve in her labor and delivery (Genesis 4:1) and to Cain as he mulls over the prospect of murdering his brother (Genesis 4:6). In other words, God is still working and speaking with humans in the fallen world, and we are still entrusted with the ongoing work of bringing to fruition the designs God has for this place. Everywhere you turn in the Bible from Genesis 1–3 and beyond, you see divine-human collaboration in a fallen world. So much of it involves word work.

## COLLABORATION THROUGHOUT THE BIBLE

At the end of this chapter, I want to come back to the idea of word work. Briefly, however, I want to focus attention on a pattern of divine-human interaction throughout the Bible: God reconfigures reality by his word and then invites us to work with him toward a goal he has in mind. Miracle is followed by collaboration. This is a central tenet of the gospel. When we read the Old Testament, we are tempted to see only the miracle part, forgetting the work that always follows it.

Take the calling of Moses as a first example. God's people had been enslaved for hundreds of years by an imperial power, Egypt, that they could never overthrow. In their misery, they cried to the Lord, and he heard them. When he decided to act on their behalf,

> The angel of the LORD appeared to [Moses] in a blazing fire from the midst of a bush. . . .
> The LORD said, "*I have surely seen* the affliction of My people who are in Egypt, and have given heed to their cry because of their taskmasters, for *I am aware* of their sufferings. So *I have come down to deliver them* from the power of the Egyptians, and to bring them up from that land to a good and spacious land."
>
> EXODUS 3:2, 7-8

Notice the italicized phrases, where the Lord seems to indicate that he is about to act *by himself* to deliver his people from Egypt. You can understand Moses' reaction when, a few sentences later, the Lord says, "Therefore, come now, and *I will send you* to Pharaoh, *so that you* may bring My people, the sons of Israel, out of Egypt" (Exodus 3:10). This created immediate tension for Moses, who responded right away with "Who am I?" (Exodus 3:11). Moses was probably thinking something like *God, you just said you had come down to deliver Israel. Why are you commissioning me to do what you intend to do? I am totally unprepared!*

Simply put, God announced a new reality to Moses ("I have come down to deliver") and then commissioned Moses to collaborate with him in it ("I will send you [to deliver]"). The opening chapters of Exodus thus mirror the opening chapters of Genesis. God does miracles we cannot do (in creation and deliverance) and then entrusts us with a share of the ongoing work. This pattern is repeated so consistently in the Bible, we are apt to miss it. We are, after all, a people capable of taking a sunrise for granted simply because it happens every day.

Think, for a moment, about the parting of the Red Sea, when the people of Israel were fleeing from the armies of Egypt. God held back the onrushing chariots of Egypt with a cloud and parted the sea with "a strong east wind all night" (Exodus 14:21). The next day, he told the Israelites to walk through it. Surely it should strike a perceptive reader that any deity capable of halting an army with a blazing pillar of fire could have simply burned them up. For that matter, any deity capable of splitting a sea in half is more than capable of moving a mass of people magically across it. He didn't need to part the sea. He didn't need to have Israel walk through it on dry ground. God prefers cooperative endeavors with his people, however. Usually, he works a miracle, then asks us to lean into its ramifications. In the case of Israel at the Red Sea, he held back the onrushing army just long enough to open a channel in the sea, then he invited Israel to walk forward.

Such was Israel's experience throughout the Exodus, the wilderness wandering, and the conquest of Canaan. Rather than doing miraculous things single-handedly, God would open horizons of possibility through providence or promise, then ask his people to trust him and move forward. This is the genius of God: His miracles draw out our faith-filled response because he delights as much in our faith as in his power. Nowhere can this be seen more clearly than in the gospel.

## THE PLACE OF THE GOSPEL
## AND THE PATTERN OF COLLABORATION

God intervenes in history to restructure reality and invites his people to respond with faith and faithfulness. This is the textual background of the Old Testament against which we should think about God's greatest work in human history: the incarnation, death, and resurrection of Jesus Christ. Like so many examples in the Old Testament, Jesus' advent and career on earth were utterly unexpected. In fact, the very idea of God coming to earth as a baby, dying as a criminal, and rising in triumph over death as Lord of all makes the Exodus from Egypt look straightforward. Even so, this miracle changed the way that people may and must relate to God and one another. Reality has been restructured around an old, rugged cross, and new horizons are now open for humanity. The New Testament refers to this new reality as "the gospel," and the writers of the New Testament believed it to be consistent with everything revealed in the Old Testament about God, the Great Collaborator.

It took everyone—even Jesus' closest followers—a while to grasp and grapple with the implications of Jesus' advent, death, and resurrection. In fact, they were still wrestling with the implications years after Jesus' ascension. I think it is fair to say that the only thing more shocking to the first generation of Jewish believers than the coming of Jesus was the coming of the Gentiles. No one expected that God would let Gentiles be saved without first converting to Judaism. When the miracle happened—when God "opened a door of faith to the Gentiles" (Acts 14:27) and filled them with his Holy Spirit without requiring them to convert to Judaism— the Jewish leaders of the church had to figure out how to respond. God was working a miracle. Now what were they to do in response?

These leaders convened in Jerusalem to listen to testimony and search the Scriptures, and we have a front-row seat to their proceedings in Acts 15. They listened as "Simeon

[Peter] . . . related how God first concerned Himself about taking from among the Gentiles a people for His name" (Acts 15:14). Though they hadn't seen it coming, they observed, "With this [testimony] the words of the Prophets agree" (Acts 15:15). In other words, God had foretold that a new reality was coming, had inaugurated it with Jesus' advent, and now was inviting his people to live into it. Thankfully, the Jewish leaders of the early church decided to collaborate with God on this one, probably because the alternative—opposing him—was unappealing.

It's easy for us to look back and wonder why it required a church council to convene fifteen years after Jesus' ascension to discuss whether Gentiles could be Christians through faith in Christ alone.[2] It helps to remember that this was a period in history when the Good News was truly *new*. It also might help to remember that no one originally thought of faith in Jesus as anything more than the fulfillment of Jewish expectations.

Up to that point, a person could only be counted among the people of God by birth or conversion. Suddenly, *everyone* had to be "born again" (John 3:3), whether Jew or Gentile, and a person could be born again without submitting to the law of Moses. This miracle we now call "the gospel" was once a conundrum. As the earliest generation of believers figured out how to lean into this new reality, entire communities began to relate to one another differently. You see this most clearly in the way they began to talk to and about one another, in their language of self-designation.

## WORDS AT WORK IN THE ADVANCEMENT OF THE GOSPEL

In 2010, I was invited to speak at the opening session of my organization's quadrennial national conference. As I was a relatively young staff person, this was a high honor, and I spent loads of time preparing the message. The text and tenor of the talk were serious, but when the moment came, I dropped a joke into my presentation that brought the house down. The laughter in that hall was uproarious, and my heart soared because I could make my friends and colleagues laugh at a "family joke." Humor is hard work, almost as hard as holiness.

It was not until the next morning, however, that I truly experienced the power of a good word spoken at the right time. The morning plenary opened with a talk from one of my heroes, Jerry Bridges. A small, soft-spoken man, Jerry was a giant to me. He always spoke with penetrating clarity about the Scriptures and the nature of God, but he always did it with humility. In his opening remarks that morning, Jerry commended me for the message I had given the night before. The commendation of this one man meant more to me than the applause and affirmation of a thousand people the night before. This is the power of the right word.

God knows how powerful the right word can be. He referred to his own Son as the Word, and he sent him at just the right time. The gospel has come down to us in the form of good words. Its terminology can sound technical at times (*reconciliation*), though it's often simple enough (*peace*).

Behind it all, though, there's a vision of reality reconfigured at the Cross and a smiling God who invites his chosen ones into a new way of living. If we want to take part in the work of shaping the world according to God's design, we will have to find ourselves at home with the words of the gospel. Proclaiming and living the gospel involves work with our words, and a huge part of this work involves figuring out what to call each other.

This is not a linguistic theory but a human observation: We don't just *say* things with words—we *do* things with them.[3] Our words have performative power. Take a striking example for starters. Go to a wedding—preferably one you've been invited to—and wait for that moment when the officiant says, "I now pronounce you man and wife." With these words, the world is changed for two people. Now they are one in the eyes of God. Even the IRS treats them differently.

A marriage ceremony is not an everyday example of words at work, of course, but it does highlight an ordinary fact. Words don't merely describe reality; they shape it. Who has not heard a parent abusing a child with hurtful words? We cringe at this not because a father is expressing his thoughts but because he is smashing a child's heart. Words can wreck worlds. This is what James meant when he said, "Think how small a flame sets a huge forest ablaze. And the tongue is a fire! . . . It is a restless evil, full of deadly poison" (James 3:5-6, 8, NET). Our words don't just describe. They can also destroy. Thanks be to God, however, they have power to create.

Our words can move people, mend relationships, and shape noble thoughts in others' minds. They can bless people and introduce them to a God who is worthy of all admiration. They can bring rivers of tears and torrents of laughter, and since humans are the only creatures on earth who laugh and cry like this, words surely have some unique power rooted in the divine image itself. Peter believed one person could speak to another "as one who speaks the very words of God . . . so that in all things God may be praised through Jesus Christ" (1 Peter 4:11, NIV). For Peter, speaking this way means we can open a channel of divine grace into the life of another person. Anyone who has heard the words "I'm sorry. Will you forgive me?" knows how powerfully this can happen.

Of course, none of us has unlimited power to shape reality with words. Only God can do that. Whatever power we have has been conferred on us. Our authority is delegated by God's good design, and we can accomplish real good or evil with the words we use. We cannot do the work that only God can do, but we can and must do the work he has entrusted to us in response to the gospel. A lot of it will be word work. This is how we can build a gospel-shaped community.

# THE FULL FORCE OF THE GOSPEL

It doesn't matter how good the performer is; you can only listen to a drum solo for so long. After three hours, Zakir Hussain, Neil Peart, and even Animal will fail to hold your attention. I wonder if that's how some of us feel about the gospel. It's incredibly good news—that's what *gospel* meant originally—but you can only listen to a message on repeat so often before you begin to tune it out.

If you have heard the gospel a time or two (or two hundred), you might agree with G. K. Chesterton that "for fallen men it is often true that familiarity is fatigue."[1] Some of us have grown fatigued with the gospel message that Jesus died to forgive us. If this is the case for you, I have good news: I'm not going to repeat that message for the next eight chapters, urging you to re-up your interest if you're serious about your faith. Instead, I'm going to suggest that you might not have heard *all* the gospel in the first place. If your gospel has been reduced to the single statement "Jesus died to forgive us," things are about to get interesting for you.

The gospel has a shape and a force that gets blunted if we oversimplify it. Don't misunderstand me. It is amazing to discover that Jesus died for our sins so that we can be forgiven. This is a message so simple a child can comprehend it yet so immense we can never master it. The notion that a holy God graciously forgives unworthy people based on faith in Christ is unparalleled. No other world religion even approaches this proclamation. If this message disappeared from the church, as it largely did in the Middle Ages, people would be left with a "gospel" that says something like this: "Honor Christ, be a good person, and pray that God grades on a curve. And invest in some of these relics in case he doesn't." The Reformation did a number on this false notion, and we are all better for it. However, the Reformation left in its wake an assertion or assumption that justification by grace through faith *is* the gospel. That's not an untrue statement, but it is an incomplete one.

## A DEFINITION OF *THE GOSPEL*

*The gospel* is a proclamation of the salvation God has accomplished for humanity through the life, death, and resurrection of Christ, as a fulfillment of the promises he made to Israel.[2] In this sense, the gospel is taught throughout both the Old and New Testaments. It is the focal point of the Bible.

What we discover about this gospel as we read the New Testament is that it doesn't just impact human hearts but also fashions new communities out of old divisions. The gospel not only says, "Your sins are forgiven." It also says, "Your family has just gotten a lot bigger!" That is precisely what the earliest generation of Christian leaders—all of them Jewish—discovered, to their own astonishment. We will take a longer look at this moment in history in the next chapter. For now, it is sufficient to say that God brought Gentiles into union with himself through the preaching of the gospel and in doing so expanded the boundary of what it means to be part of the people of God.

The gospel, then, involves God's decision to reshape not just souls but societies around Christ, as a fulfillment of his promises to Israel. What is more, the gospel tells us that the fatal powers of Satan, sin, and death have been defeated at the Cross. This is more than a message of forgiveness. It is a declaration of the victory of God through the incarnation, death, resurrection, and ascension of Israel's long-awaited Messiah.

These are the ideas known to us as justification, redemption, and reconciliation. When we find them in Scripture, they are rarely standing alone. Take this example from Romans 5:

While we were still helpless, at the right time Christ
died for the ungodly. For one will hardly die for
a righteous man; though perhaps for the good
man someone would dare even to die. But God
demonstrates His own love toward us, in that while
we were yet sinners, Christ died for us. Much more
then, having now been justified by His blood, we
shall be saved from the wrath of God through Him.
For if while we were enemies we were reconciled
to God through the death of His Son, much more,
having been reconciled, we shall be saved by His life.

ROMANS 5:6-10

Though this passage is very short, you get a clear picture of
multiple gospel forces at work. Forgiveness, power, and peace
all flow from the grace of God into the life of a Christian
because of the Cross. The problem is not that the text in
front of us is unclear but that we have had a tendency since
the time of the Reformation to amplify the message about
justification and mute the significance of redemption and
reconciliation.

I have no interest in downplaying the doctrine of justification. Who would want to mute the message that God in
his mercy sent Jesus to bear our sins on the Cross and die in
our place so that we do not have to endure eternal wrath? The
sins that were rightly ours to bear throughout eternity were
laid on Jesus, and the righteous life he lived is reckoned to
our account. All this is by the grace of God. We didn't earn

it, nor do we deserve it. We are saved by grace through faith in Christ alone.

This *is* the gospel! However, it is not *all* the gospel. The gospel is not *less than* this message of justification, but it is *more than* this message. If I'm correct in this assessment, there are depths to the gospel many of us have yet to discover, dimensions to it that might surprise us. But there's more than just the thrill of discovery at stake here. I'm concerned that an imbalance in our gospel has overworked justification while overlooking the doctrines of redemption and, especially, reconciliation. If the gospel is like a three-engine jet, we are attempting to fly the evangelical plane on one engine. A trijet can maintain its trajectory with only one engine, but it will immediately lose altitude and must find a place to land soon. Losing two engines turns a trijet into a long-range glider.

## THE GOSPEL IS A MIRACLE THAT RESHAPES THE REALITY WE LIVE INTO

A gospel that soars on all three engines makes clear to confused minds and broken hearts *what God has already done* for us through the life, death, and resurrection of Christ, along with *what we have yet to accomplish* with him by his grace. Most of us have heard that we *receive* the righteousness of Christ through faith. We do not *earn* it. This is a core component of the doctrine of justification. Our innocent standing before God comes to us by grace through faith in

Jesus, not through our works for him. Paul says it this way: "He saved us, not on the basis of deeds which we have done in righteousness, but according to His mercy, by the washing of regeneration and renewing by the Holy Spirit" (Titus 3:5).

The *consequence* of this salvation that God has accomplished on our behalf is that we do, in fact, grow in holiness. We pursue righteousness in our daily lives because we have been made righteous at the Cross of Christ. Good works flow from our salvation like water from a spring. There would be no water downstream were it not for the water at the source. Righteousness conferred on the ill deserving is the water at the source. Righteousness in daily living is the downstream effect. The water doesn't flow uphill. This is precisely the pattern we observed in the previous chapter: God works on our behalf to create realities we could not create—in this case, our righteous standing—and then invites us to live into them—in this case, our righteous living. I hope you have heard an explanation like this of the nature and effects of justification everywhere the gospel has been preached.

What I want you to understand is that the wellspring of our salvation—the water at the source—consists of more than justification. There are at least three decisive acts of God in salvation that comprise the gospel as it is announced in the New Testament: justification, redemption, and reconciliation.[3] The latter two are not tributaries of the first. Rather, they all represent *different aspects* of God's *one work* of salvation. All three have been accomplished by the grace of God on our behalf at the Cross of Christ, and all three have downstream effects in the lives of believers. All three represent the miracle of salvation and define the new reality believers get to live into. For ease of reference (and at the risk of oversimplifying things myself!), I will outline them below:

### Justification
- addresses the problem of our *guilt*
- speaks primarily in terms of "forgiveness" and "righteousness"
- changes our relationship to God, self, and others with respect to the law and the dictates of conscience

### Redemption
- addresses the problem of our *bondage*
- speaks primarily in terms of "freedom" and "power"
- changes our relationship to God, self, and others with respect to the authority of Satan, Sin, and Death[4]

### Reconciliation
- addresses the problem of *enmity*
- speaks primarily in terms of "peace" and "union"
- changes our relationship to God, self, and others with respect to our hostility and apathy

As I mentioned, these three categories of justification, redemption, and reconciliation are never presented in the New Testament hermetically sealed from one another. You will rarely find a passage that isolates one of them and analyzes only its effects. For instance, forgiveness is a central concept in justification, but it also appears in a luminous passage about redemption (Ephesians 1:7). Meanwhile, it's impossible to think about reconciliation between hostile parties without forgiveness coming into play. These concepts share an organic relationship with one another as close as the bonds of electrons, protons, and neutrons (more on that below). They are logically distinguishable, but they constitute the one thing we call "the gospel." They refer to different dimensions or forces of the work of God in salvation, forces that work themselves out powerfully in the lives and relationships we share.

Although I haven't studied chemistry (or physics) since the late 1980s, I think atoms are still regarded as the smallest stable units of matter. If you knock the electron out of an atom, you no longer have the same atom but an isotope or a different atom or a free ion floating around wondering what just happened. "A free ion," Albert Einstein probably wrote somewhere, "is kind of like a teenage boy: an unstable, negative particle roaming about the universe looking for a positive force to attach himself to." It's only when the electrons, protons, and neutrons have all situated themselves into stable bonds that you have an atom. The gospel is like that.

The work of God in Christ to rescue humans may be understood as three cooperating forces that comprise the one thing we call salvation. If you want to grasp the gospel, it is best to understand all these constituent parts in their harmonious combination. You can focus your attention on one aspect of the gospel to understand its nature and behavior, but the gospel will always be more than that one constituent part. A gospel that always and only focuses on one of these forces will be imbalanced, and if we believe in an imbalanced gospel, we won't experience the fullness of the gospel's power to transform lives.

## HOW GOSPEL FORCES INFLUENCE OUR LIVES

For the past twenty years, I have worked with college students who are living with sexually compulsive behaviors or pornography addictions. I have consistently told the people who come to me for help that they need a fellow traveler who can preach the gospel to them in their personal darkness, speak with moral authority, and offer wise guidance about what steps to take next. I want you to focus on that first criterion only: What would it mean to preach the gospel to someone who has been compulsively using porn and masturbating for a decade or more?

If our gospel only spoke to us about justification, here is what we would probably say to others: "Though you have sinned, God has declared you (and me!) innocent because Jesus bore our sins on the Cross. What is more, in our wretchedness, God sees us clothed in the righteousness of Christ. Where our sin is greatest, God's grace is greater still." This is the gospel! How many people burdened by years of treachery toward God and the ones they love need to hear this! So many people have never heard it at all.

If you believe this message is true, preach it to yourself

and others with all your heart. I want you to consider another question, however: *If the gospel* also *says that Jesus set me free from slavery to sin, Satan, and death at the Cross, what else should I be communicating?* Could we not say just as boldly that no Christian should believe or live as though sin has greater power to enslave than Jesus has to liberate? That Jesus has, in fact and for all who believe in him, shattered the dominion of Satan for all time at the Cross? That our own desperate weakness is the very platform on which God longs to display his perfect power? This, too, is the gospel!

When I began to grasp this dimension of the gospel, I started asking three diagnostic questions any time a person came to me struggling with porn. (People generally use the euphemism "I am struggling with porn" to mean "My heart and all my hopes are being hollowed out by a habit that has become a private hell. I hate myself, and I seem to drag almost everyone I encounter into the constricting sphere of my own self-love and self-loathing.") When such a person comes to me now, I ask these three questions:

1. Do you believe God can set *a person* free from the sins that enslave them?
2. Do you believe that God can set *you* free from your bondage?
3. Are you willing to do whatever it takes to experience this freedom?

These questions point people toward the gospel force of redemption. I remember sitting on the steps of Huff Hall at the University of Illinois with a student who wanted to join a support group I was leading. When I asked him whether he believed God could set *a person* free from the compulsive use of porn and masturbation, he said yes without hesitation. When I looked at him and asked, "Do you think God can set *you* free?" he began to weep uncontrollably. It took him several minutes to compose himself enough to whisper, "But I have tried and tried, and nothing has ever worked."

What does your gospel have to say to such a person at such a time? It *has* to say more than "You have been forgiven at the Cross of Christ." It needs to say, "You have been set free at the Cross of Christ" and "God has brought you and me together at the Cross of Christ so that we can walk forward through this." The gospel proclaims the promise of forgiveness *and* freedom *and* peace. If the gospel only announced good news about forgiveness, we might well have no answer to the objection "So what do we do? Keep on sinning so God can keep on forgiving?" (Romans 6:1, MSG). When Paul faced this very objection, he did not double down on the doctrine of justification that he had been hammering out in Romans 1–5. Instead, he parried the challenge to one dimension of the gospel (justification) by highlighting the other two (redemption and reconciliation).

In Romans 6:5 and 6:7, Paul says *it simply could never be* that people assured of forgiveness would go on sinning *because* we "have become united with [Christ]" (reconciliation) in his life and death and we have been "freed from sin" (redemption).[5] Paul is holding out union and freedom—redemption and reconciliation—as the reason people who know they are justified will not go on sinning. In doing so, Paul parries a challenge to *one* dimension of the gospel by emphatically proclaiming *all* dimensions of it. He foregrounds every force of the gospel as a more than adequate answer to the cynicism, sin, and suffering of this fallen world.

In the next chapter, I'm going to focus more attention on the gospel force of reconciliation. I want to move it into the foreground for you because it has been backgrounded in the church. By the end of the next chapter, I hope you will agree that God has not only reconciled you to himself but also to all who are in Christ. This is a finished work, a miracle of grace, and we get to experience its fullness as we build gospel-shaped communities. What we're about to discover is that this message is preached repeatedly in every letter of the New Testament, but many of us have missed it. The gospel of reconciliation has been hiding in plain sight.

# THE REALITY OF RECONCILIATION

In 2007, I took an Amtrak train from central Illinois to Union Station in Chicago. I grew up in small-town America, so this was an auspicious occasion for me. I was heading into the heart of a big city I had always bypassed by driving through Rockford, and I was going to get a first look at the iconic Sears Tower (now the Willis Tower). When I got off the train in the bowels of Union Station, I had no idea how to get out. Never one to ask for help, I followed a crowd of people up a random escalator and emerged onto a bustling street. For all I knew, any building above me at that moment could have been the Sears Tower. But how could I be sure? They all looked equally imposing.

Too proud to ask anyone, I decided to walk the whole circumference of Union Station (it takes up ten blocks) and figure it out myself. I kept glancing at the sky, gawking at the crowds, and trying to figure out why everyone honked their horns continuously. I finally decided that the buildings close to the station were probably blocking my view of the Sears Tower, so I expanded my perimeter. I walked and walked the blocks around Union Station, glancing up periodically, trying not to get run over. I read the signs on the tall buildings, but I never found one that said Sears Tower.

Eventually, I made my way back to Union and sat on a wall by the canal to eat a Chicago-style hot dog and a donut. Soon enough, a middle-aged man planted himself on the wall beside me. I decided it was time to break my self-imposed silence.

"Excuse me," I said. "Could you tell me where the Sears Tower is?"

The man looked at me for an awkward second, then stretched his arm out over the canal and pointed a finger upward. The Sears Tower could hardly have been more obvious if had been painted pink. It literally towered above every building near it.

I still have no idea why I could not see the Sears Tower that day. Some people who have heard the story assume I am making it up. People who know me well know better. I am capable of monumental oversights. This one, however, represented one of my most spectacular accomplishments. I can only assume that God needed to send a message to the guy sitting on the wall next to me. Maybe he needed a good laugh or a good story to tell his kids. He certainly got a living parable: Sometimes a thing impossible to miss can be hard to see. Even the Sears Tower can hide in plain sight from a bumpkin on stimulus overload.

The gospel force of reconciliation may be hiding in plain sight on the pages of the New Testament. Ask a seasoned Christian or an avid new believer to tell you about reconciliation, and they will (I hope) say that God has made friends of those who were once his enemies through the death and resurrection of Christ. Ask them where they discovered that in the Bible, and they might have to search a little bit. Go one step further and ask them what this gospel of reconciliation has to say about our relationships *with each other*, and they may be stumped. They will probably start talking about how we *ought to behave* in relationship with one another to build constructive communities. That message is not exactly the gospel, however. Every world religion and everyone's common sense says that we should love one another, try to be patient with each other, and so on. The gospel does not beckon us to create a community we don't have. It welcomes us into the one God created for his glory and our good right here on earth, lasting for all eternity.

## RECONCILIATION IN REVERSE

If you search for *reconciliation* in the Gospels and Acts (the narrative portions of the New Testament), you'll find that the word only shows up twice. In the Sermon on the Mount, Jesus talks about the need to be reconciled to your brother if you remember that he has something against you when you are going to offer a sacrifice (see Matthew 5:23-24). Stephen also uses the word *reconciliation* when he talks about Moses' attempt to settle a quarrel between Israelites in Egypt (see Acts 7:26). In both cases, the parties in conflict must recognize their share in the wrongs they have committed and take steps to rectify the situation. That's typically the way we think of reconciliation: A person responsible for a wrong takes appropriate steps to make it right with the one who's been wronged. When we come to Paul's writings, however, we find that he uses the word very differently—so differently, in fact, that it looks like reconciliation is working in reverse.

In Paul's teaching, God takes the initiative to reconcile relationships with people *who have wronged him*. This is peculiar. In fact, it would have been a wild notion in the wider Greco-Roman world for anyone to talk about a god being reconciled to a person. *Reconciliation* is an inescapably *relational* word, and people did not think of gods sharing this kind of relationship with humans. Greek philosophers, poets, and priests might have talked about appeasing or placating a god but not about reconciling a relationship with one, much less about a god reconciling a relationship with you! When it came to appeasing a god, everything was up to the needy person. The burden fell on us, the wrongdoers, the weaker partners. Paul thought and taught the opposite about God: God wanted a reconciled relationship with sinful and weak people, so he took matters into his own hands and made it happen.

Throughout the Scriptures, we find example after example of God moving toward unworthy humans, not with hostility but with resolve to overcome the chasm between them. In doing so, he brings peace to people who deserve wrath. We have glanced at Romans 5 before, but it's worth considering it again in light of the distinct emphasis Paul places on *who takes the initiative* to overcome the hostility subsisting between God and sinners:

> You see, at just the right time, *when we were still powerless*, Christ died for the ungodly. . . . But God demonstrates his own love for us in this: *While we were still sinners*, Christ died for us.
>
> Since we have now been justified by his blood, how much more shall we be saved from God's wrath through him! For if, *while we were God's enemies*, we were reconciled to him through the death of his Son, how much more, having been reconciled, shall we be saved through his life! Not only is this so, but we also boast in God through our Lord Jesus Christ, through whom we have now received reconciliation.
>
> ROMANS 5:6, 8-11, NIV

What Paul is describing here is what I call "reconciliation in reverse." Though he has done no wrong, God takes unilateral action to make peace with those who have done him wrong *while they are still in the wrong*. The enmity we put between ourselves and God because of our sins God removed at the Cross of Christ. We *receive reconciliation* from God through faith in the Lord Jesus Christ. We do not reconcile ourselves. That is why our peace with God will last for eternity.

## UNITED WITH CHRIST AND ALL WHO ARE IN CHRIST

Nothing in heaven or on earth "will be able to separate us from the love of God, which is in Christ Jesus our Lord" (Romans 8:39). Because of our union with Christ, believers may live with the eternal assurance that God will deal with us only and always as he would his own Son. I have always appreciated the way Jerry Bridges has explained this union in his book *Trusting God*:

> We are constantly tempted to look within ourselves
> to seek to find some reason why God should love us.
> Such searching is, of course, usually discouraging.
> We usually find within ourselves reasons why we
> think God should *not* love us. Such searching is
> also unbiblical. The Bible is quite clear that God
> does not look within us for a reason to love us. He
> loves us because we are in Christ Jesus. When He
> looks at us, He does not look at us as "stand alone"
> Christians, resplendent in our own good works, even
> good works as Christians. Rather, as He looks at us,

He sees us united to His beloved Son, clothed in His righteousness. He loves us, not because we are lovely in ourselves, but because we are in Christ.[1]

We are not "stand alone" Christians. Though we are called "new creature[s]" in 2 Corinthians 5:17, we have not been recreated as new "stand alone" beings. Rather, the passage says that "if anyone is *in Christ*, he is a new creature; the old things passed away; behold, new things have come. Now all these things are from God, who *reconciled us to Himself through Christ*" (2 Corinthians 5:17-18). God regards us as new creatures by virtue of our union with his Son.

If we started reading this passage in its larger context, we would see another angle on reconciliation that may be hiding in plain sight. Paul's larger point in 2 Corinthians 5 is that we should accustom ourselves to think of *other* people (not ourselves) as *potential* new creatures because of the potential of the gospel to transform every person. Every sinner may be reconciled to God in Christ, and this means every human community may be radically realigned.

Union with Christ does not simply change *my* relationship with God. It changes our relationships with one another. The unbridgeable gap of enmity between us and God was spanned by the Cross, and the peace that results from this union will be *never-ending*. More than this, the reconciliation of the Cross will be *ever extending* because God brings into new relationship with us everyone who has been brought into new relationship with him. This is how Paul explains the phenomenon in Ephesians (small caps represent a quotation from the Old Testament):

> But now in Christ Jesus you who formerly were far off have been brought near by the blood of Christ. For He Himself is our peace, who made both groups [Jews and Gentiles] into one and broke down the barrier of the dividing wall, by abolishing in His flesh the enmity, which is the Law of commandments contained in ordinances, so that in Himself He might make the two into one new man, thus establishing peace, and might reconcile them both in one body to God through the cross, by it having put to death the enmity. AND HE CAME AND PREACHED PEACE TO YOU WHO WERE FAR AWAY, AND PEACE TO THOSE WHO WERE NEAR; for through Him we both have our access in one Spirit to the Father. So then you are no longer strangers and aliens, but you are fellow citizens with the saints, and are of God's household.
>
> EPHESIANS 2:13-19

Writing to an audience of predominantly Gentile Christians, Paul says there was once a time when they had no place among the people of God, the Jews. Nevertheless, in Christ, they have become "fellow citizens with the saints, and are of God's household" (Ephesians 2:19). How did this reconciliation take place? They did not believe in the Jewish

Messiah *and* convert to Judaism (or vice versa). They simply put their faith in Jesus, the Jewish Messiah, and God made them one people with Jewish believers. They were, quite literally, brought together in the body of Christ at the Cross. The two groups who were formerly hostile to one another, separated by law and culture, history and blood, were made into "one new man" (Ephesians 2:15) through faith in Jesus. In bringing these two groups to God, Jesus also brought them together. They are now one new person. Through his sacrifice, Jesus established peace in heaven and on earth.

It is precisely here that we are tempted to think of this peace on earth as "potential peace" between people. The evidence before our eyes says that we still have a long way to go in living harmoniously with others in the church. While this is true (in its way), it is not the gospel. The gospel always speaks to us about a finished work of Christ at the Cross that opens up new potential. Peace between separated communities is part of the finished work of Christ, not merely the future potential of Christ's people. The harmony that defines your relationship with all other Christians is just as full and final as the peace Jesus established between you and God. That peace may be realized in a hundred different ways and unrealized in a hundred others. You do not complete the reconciling work of Christ on the Cross, however. You receive it and live into its reality.

Believers in Jesus do not become family—"of God's household" (Ephesians 2:19), as Paul put it—through ongoing effort but through faith in Christ. We do not relate to other believers in a certain way to *become* one people but *because* we already are. The work of Jesus is decisive and complete. Of course, this cannot possibly mean we have nothing left to do. That would also be false to the gospel and the pattern we have observed throughout Scripture (which can be seen in chapter 1 of this book). All the miracles of God set up corresponding collaboration. We walk and work with God to fulfill his designs. God parts the Red Sea, and his people walk through it. In this case, the gospel tells us we have much to do *now that we are a family.* We must begin at the beginning, however: In Christ, God has already done for us what we couldn't do for ourselves so that we can now do what he has always wanted done.

God has brought all believers together in a household they *could not have created* but *must now preserve.* Paul uses this very language when he commands believers "to walk in a manner worthy of the calling with which you have been called, with all humility and gentleness, with patience, showing tolerance for one another in love, being diligent *to preserve the unity of the Spirit in the bond of peace*" (Ephesians 4:1-3). Christians do not aspire to a unity they do not possess; they express a unity that has already been won. This is the gospel message of reconciliation.

## RECONCILIATION IN THE REGISTER OF RELATIONSHIP

If you scan the New Testament for the word *reconciliation*, you will only find thirteen occurrences outside the Gospels.

That may be slightly disappointing after I have hyped up this force of the gospel in so many paragraphs. But remember, I have said that the message of reconciliation may be hiding in plain sight. If you randomly flip open your Bible to any letter in the New Testament, do you see words like *brother*, *sister*, *children*, or *household* there? What about *saints* ("God's holy people")? Or *beloved*? On page after page of the New Testament, we come away with the unmistakable impression that the first generation of Christians believed they were one family, one people, one body. They don't spend a lot of time describing the nature of their relationship. They declare it!

I call this the proclamation of reconciliation in the register of relationship. That is, when Christians spoke to one another or about themselves as a community, they spoke in common terms of close relationship. The people around them would have found their references to one another as "brothers and sisters" very odd because that's simply not how people talked across boundaries of ethnicity and class in the Greco-Roman or Jewish worlds (and there were massive boundaries of ethnicity and class in the ancient world).

Take the city of (Syrian) Antioch, for example, where "the disciples were first called Christians" (Acts 11:26). In the fourth century, it was the fourth largest city of the Roman Empire. Sociologist Rodney Stark, who studied the rise of Christianity, described it as a city populated by "Syrians . . . Greeks . . . retired soldiers from Seleucus's Macedonian army, Cretans, Cypriotes, Argives, and Herakleidae . . . Athenians from Atigonia, Jews from nearby Palestine . . . a number of slaves of diverse origins . . . Romans . . . Gauls, Germans and other 'barbarians.'"[2] That is a roll call of very different people living in very difficult surroundings. Here is how Stark characterizes the conditions in the city:

> Any accurate portrait of Antioch in New Testament times must depict a city filled with misery, danger, fear, despair, and hatred. A city where the average family lived a squalid life in filthy and cramped quarters, where at least half of the children died at birth or during infancy, and where most of the children who lived lost at least one parent before reaching maturity. A city filled with hatred and fear rooted in intense ethnic antagonisms and exacerbated by a constant stream of strangers. A city so lacking in stable networks of attachments that petty incidents could prompt mob violence.[3]

If you walked into a house church in Antioch during the first century, what kinds of people would you have found there? We do not have records, but we can make an educated guess: You would likely find refugees, immigrants, rich people, poor people, prostitutes, shop owners, slave owners, slaves, Jews, Greeks, Gauls, Romans, and so on. The gospel had not simply thrown together people with different theological perspectives on God. It had bound together people with nothing in common except Jesus Christ himself. Knowing this, we can begin to grasp how odd it was for any religion to say to all these people, "You are now brothers and sisters because the Son of God was executed and rose from the dead!"

When Paul proclaimed the gospel and founded churches in the urban centers of the Roman Empire, he brought together people deeply divided by socioeconomic and ethnic fissures that defined every aspect of their everyday lives. Of all people, Paul knew what this was like. As a zealous Pharisee in Roman-occupied territory, he knew how impervious religious and ethnic barriers could be. So how was the gospel to bring such people together? Even granted that they shared some mystic, spiritual union through Christ, how were they to be practically united as a family on earth?

The answer might be simpler than you think, hiding in plain sight: People in the early church started calling one another what they were. If you walked into their assemblies or sat with them at mealtimes, you would hear them call each other "brothers and sisters" or "beloved." They would refer to their community as "saints," "disciples," and "fellow workers." In other words, they spoke to one another in a certain register of belonging. A register is not a different language or even a different dialect. It's just a peculiar way of speaking or writing within certain social settings to signal closeness or distance.

I realize no one uses the word *register* in normal life, unless you happen to hang out with linguists. (And if you hang out with linguists, there's a good chance your life is not very normal.) Even so, knowing how registers function helps us understand how the gospel of reconciliation was proclaimed in the early church. To get there, let's take a familiar example. Listen to yourself pray. Almost everyone who's been around the church for any length of time develops a "prayer register," one they pick up from the other people praying around them. For some, this involves addressing God as "Lord," "God," or "Father" (or "Lord, Father God") *a lot* in one stretch of discourse. This is not a problem—it's a register. It's a reasonably well-defined way of talking to God with others around to show that you (all) respect him.

There's never been a time, however, when you would address a friend, Pam, by calling her "Pam" ten times in a brief conversation. We may do this all the time with God in prayer, but we would never do this with Pam in the living room. This is not a criticism; it's just an observation. In fact, I'd be willing to bet that you would address the king of England as "Your Highness" more times than you would call Pam "Pam" if you ever had an audience with the king. That's because certain social settings invite us to adopt registers to reveal *where we stand in relation to others.* These are verbal markers of social distance or closeness, and they are important for navigating relational space, especially unfamiliar spaces or ones where power differentials are especially great.

The prayer register we have learned is part of the way we show respect for God because he is so great. The more familiar we become with a register, the less we notice it, however. You probably don't think too much about how the people in your church pray until a new person comes in who doesn't know the routine. Often, when a new believer (or nonbeliever) prays, they sound so . . . *normal*. They have not learned the language patterns your group has developed for addressing God, so they just talk to him as one person might talk to another. When they do so, you probably think, *That was so refreshing! It sounded so normal.* At the same time, the visitor probably thought, *That was so awkward! I have no idea how I'm supposed to talk out loud to an invisible deity with a group of people listening.*

You might have liked the way the newcomer's prayer showed intimacy with God. They might have felt uncomfortable because they didn't know how to show respect to God when talking aloud to him. Regardless of how either of you felt initially, there will be one outcome if the stranger joins your group: They will start to sound like you do when they pray. It will happen so slowly no one will notice, but give them a few months, and they will begin addressing the invisible God out loud the way your group does. That's because registers are a social phenomenon that we learn when we join a group. They help us know how to communicate *in a social setting* to signal how close or distant we are to others.

You might wonder what would happen if no one in your group had a prayer register because all of you were new. The answer is quite easy: You would develop one. The same is true for all communication in all social groups that meet regularly. It is not possible to gather regularly with the same group of people without developing unofficial, but very definite, protocols for communicating.

This is precisely what happened in the time of the New Testament. People with little in common were suddenly meeting to pray, eat dinner, and discuss the apostles' teaching. In short order, they developed patterned ways of talking *to* and *about* one other, the language of self-designation, a social register that signaled their social closeness. The pattern is so clear, we can see it in their letters two thousand years later!

There is a chance that most Christians in the first century would have struggled to explain the doctrine of reconciliation in *theological* terms. (It is certain that many Christians in the twenty-first century cannot.) If you were to listen to them, however, you would hear them express the doctrine in *relational* terms. They used common words in uncommon ways. Jews called Gentiles "brothers and sisters" in the church. Slave owners called their slaves "beloved." The doctrine of reconciliation was being preached in the register of relationship. Jesus had changed the structure of human society, and the churches reflected it in the way they spoke about one another. As British scholar John Barclay says, these were "outrageously novel applications of biblical terms and categories [within] a new multi-ethnic community."[4]

What we discover as we survey the early history of the Christian movement is that their registers of relationship worked! They told the truth about who they were in relationship to one another, and they changed the world. That is, everywhere believers gathered, they declared the gospel of reconciliation. Everywhere the gospel was preached, more lives were changed.

These words could work in the same way today as they did in the first century. The New Testament has bequeathed to history a rich register of reconciliation. If we will think and talk in these terms, we will invariably express, experience, and expand the work of the gospel.

As I write this chapter, I am conscious of how polarized the church in the United States has become along political and ideological fault lines. Many Christians have found that they cannot even have civil conversations in their own biological families about policies or candidates. Conversations in churches are no different unless the whole church happens to vote the same ticket and listen to the same podcasts. Many people trumpet their political allegiance far more assertively than they do their Christian unity. We seem determined to widen the gaps between us. I think there is a better way forward in the church, and it requires no argument or caveats about where we stand politically. We can simply call fellow Christians "my brother" and "my sister." Of course, if we adopt the family language of the New Testament, we'd better be prepared for the consequences. The early church set a good example.

You don't have to master doctrinal concepts to do this work. You don't even have to know the term *register* or have a theory about how language shapes community. You simply need to begin addressing fellow believers as something more than "Christians." Ordinary people using common words in uncommon ways to express extraordinary realities changes the world. This simple fact is startling: Before we were

"Christians," we knew what to call each other. We used the language of "brothers and sisters," "beloved," "saints," "disciples," and "fellow workers." These were the earliest words that strengthened the social bonds Jesus had forged across cultural gaps at the Cross. For hundreds of years, Christians declared the gospel of reconciliation in the register of relationship. Today, we might *think* in these terms, but we generally use one of them—"Christians"—in conversation. I hope we might change this pattern. I think our world would be better for it.

# BROTHERS AND SISTERS IN THE TIME OF THE NEW TESTAMENT

As we discussed in the previous chapter, the New Testament writers preached a gospel of reconciliation in the register of relationship.[1] They used common terms in uncommon ways to express how close their relationships had become in Christ. By far, their preferred term of self-designation was "brothers and sisters."[2] Christians used this expression when they addressed one another directly, and they described one another this way frequently. If you scan the Bible quickly or skim it casually, you can't miss this fact. If you take this fact for granted, however, you will almost certainly miss one of the most stupendous miracles of the Bible: Nothing had ever brought people together like the gospel. Nothing proclaimed this gospel more clearly than the words Christians used to talk *to* and *about* one another.

Words do not merely describe things. They work magic, and we are all magicians. We have all learned intuitively how to signal and strengthen relationships with the words we use. (For that matter, we also know how to create distance with our words or our silence.) We shape our social world with simple syllables. Every time my teenage son uses the word *bro* in a conversation with a friend on his basketball team, he's working with word magic. The fact that he never uses this word with me . . . also part of the magic. Consider the following everyday examples of the way we signal and shape social distance and closeness with our words.

## WRITING YOUR WAY INTO SOCIAL DISTANCE

*To Whom It May Concern:*

*I am writing today to inquire about the application I submitted to your office two weeks ago. I am eager to work as an intern at Knobby Plastic Parts Inc. this summer. I think you will find my strengths and experience well suited to Knobby's mission and workplace culture. I hope to hear from you soon and would welcome any chance to prove that I am more than qualified for the position.*

*Love,*
*Norman Hubbard*

This sample email is not copyright protected. Feel free to use it yourself if you are applying for a new job, *as long as you delete the closing*! No one would ever write a letter this formal that begins with "To Whom It May Concern" only to end it with "Love, Norman." From the opening salutation to the last sentence, everything is calculated to create respectful social distance—the kind you would expect to find in a job application. Everything feels right until the closing. You don't end a formal appeal like a love note.

Take another example from your school days. There is a very good chance you did not refer to many teachers in your kindergarten-through–twelfth grade days by their first names. You might have called them any number of nick-names behind their backs, but to their faces, you probably called them "Mr." or "Ms." Take my eleventh-grade physics teacher, for example. His name was Mr. Faile. (True story. You can't make this stuff up.) To this day, I have no idea what Mr. Faile's first name was. Or whether he had one. The thought of trying to discover his name would have felt like necromancy. Uttering it might have bound you to repeat eleventh-grade physics for the rest of your life. If Mr. Faile had a first name, I never knew it, and if I had, I never would have used it.

Of course, my dad might have known Mr. Faile's first name. He might have even called Mr. Faile "Jerry" at the American Legion pancake breakfast. No dark incantation there. That's simply how word magic works in social relation-ships. Simple, sometimes imperceptible, differences in the way we address people say everything we need to know about where we stand in relation to one another.

A big part of our informal education in life involves learning the dynamics of creating social distance with different audiences. We mimic the patterns we observe and repeat them unconsciously. No one has to lecture us for long on proper ways to address people. The more stable the social setting, the more readily we learn our place in it. Unfamiliar social settings or deliberate breaches of protocol in familiar ones leave us feeling tense. Nowhere did I feel this tension more than in marriage, a third and final example of direct address (but one that deserves a section of its own).

## "MR. AND MRS. HANSEN"

When I was a kid growing up down South, my mom always referred to her in-laws as "Mr. and Mrs. Hubbard." My parents both grew up in the small town of Talladega, Alabama, where every adult was a "Mr." or "Mrs." to anyone younger. For my mom, this natural marker of social respect carried over into married life. The rest of the world may have called my dad's parents "Cowboy and Virginia Hubbard," but they were always "Mr. and Mrs. Hubbard" to her. I saw nothing strange about this when I was a kid. Perhaps there is nothing that *can* seem strange to you when your granddaddy's name is Cowboy.[3]

It was not until I married Katie Hansen that I discovered there was another way of talking to your in-laws. Katie and I first began to date in college, and I naturally referred to her parents as "Mr. and Mrs. Hansen." The Hansens were from Wisconsin, but we were all living in Alabama at the time. We all knew the drill: Young people call their elders "Mr." or "Mrs." Things got decidedly less natural a few months after Katie and I were married, however. Mrs. Hansen made a simple request.

"Please do not call us 'Mr. and Mrs.' any longer," she said. "We are your parents-in-law now."

I was dumbfounded by this statement. I had continued calling them "Mr. and Mrs." precisely *because* they were my in-laws. *What alternative do I have?* I wondered.

"Just call us 'Mom' and 'Dad,'" Mrs. Hansen went on.

I have no idea what my face looked like when my mother-in-law suggested this. I probably stared at her like she had asked me to prepare a dish of falafel from a cookbook written in Farsi. There was no way I could do what she was asking. I couldn't call my in-laws "Mom and Dad" any more than I could long jump the Grand Canyon. I told my wife as much later. I only had one mom and dad. I liked her parents a lot, but they were my in-laws, not my "mom and dad."

I had assumed the slow-growing familiarity I had enjoyed with Katie's mom and dad would never evolve beyond slow-growing familiarity and the formal bounds of "Mr. and Mrs. Hansen." (It never had for my mom. Why should it be any different for me?) My in-laws took the opposite view, however. They assumed their relationship with me would progressively look and feel—and sound!—like the relationship they had with their three biological sons. Thankfully, "Mrs. Hansen" could sense how awkward this was for me, and she didn't push things.

My in-laws bore with my formality for years until I finally brought myself around to calling them "Mom and Dad." I don't even remember how the change took place. I only remember that while I was calling them "Mr. and Mrs. Hansen," Katie's mom would sign cards and letters to me with "Your Mother-in-Love" or "Mom II." Her persistence in relating to me as a son finally paid off. One day, I called them "Mom and Dad," and I have never looked back. The longer I called them "Mom and Dad," the closer I felt to them. The words we were using gave a certain shape to our relationship.

Years later, my relationship with my in-laws underwent the strain and sorrow of losing Katie to cancer. After twenty-one years of marriage, Katie went home to be with the Lord while we were living in her parents' home. We had just moved to Wisconsin because Katie's health was failing fast, and we were waiting for our new home to be built. Katie died on January 25, 2016. That night, I spent my first night alone in my in-laws' home. What a mercy that Mr. and Mrs. Hansen had become "Mom and Dad" to me. Two decades earlier, they had decided I would be their "son." I was not a stranger or a "son-in-law" to them when I needed family most. I was, quite simply, their son.

Over and over since that day in January, they have

reaffirmed this relationship. "You are our son. You always will be," they will say. That is why this book is dedicated to them. Mom and Dad Hansen showed me by word and deed that family can mean something more than blood. The earliest generation of Christians discovered the same thing in the same way.

## LEARNING TO ADDRESS ONE ANOTHER AS FAMILY

What "Mr. and Mrs. Hansen" taught me about the nature of family the earliest generation of believers learned from the apostles. As members of newly forming communities who had faith in Jesus as Lord, they had to figure out what to call each other. They landed on the term *brothers and sisters*.[4]

There's a profound practicality to figuring this kind of thing out, of course. You have to know how to hail someone in the marketplace or greet them at a dinner party. This is especially true in a new social setting. The thing we cannot miss—and the thing we are prone to miss when the New Testament language gets taken for granted—is that the first generation of Christians worked magic when they landed on the term *brothers and sisters*. World-shaping work was done when the earliest generation of Christians started identifying each other as family.

We must remember that in the early days of the church, *no conventions* existed for how Jews and Gentiles, rich and poor, men and women would address one another. There was no register for people to drop into. There were other communities similar to Christian churches, of course. People could join trade guilds, mystery cults, ethnic associations, and synagogues almost anywhere in the Greco-Roman world. All these groups formed along lines of natural affinity, ancestry, or practical need, however. People chose a guild because they all worked the same craft. People joined a neighborhood association because they lived on the same street (and usually came from the same ethnic group). Christians, however, assembled for a different reason. All they had in common was Christ. They were sitting together in one room because they had come together at one Cross. For most of them, there weren't multiple options for where to worship. Their union in Christ wasn't an idea or an ideal but a practical reality. It was an entirely new social situation though. What were they supposed to call each other before they were "Christians"?

All the evidence of the New Testament and beyond says their most common term of self-designation was "brothers and sisters." It should not take enormous mental effort for us to imagine how awkward this must have felt at first for people so obviously *not* related (and, in fact, even hostile) to one another. Yet this is precisely what they did.

The writers of the New Testament directly addressed other believers as "brothers and sisters" seventy-seven times outside the Gospels. Though *you* may be familiar with some of these verses, none would have seemed normal when they were first read aloud in the first century:

Brothers and Sisters in the Time of the New Testament

Therefore, I urge you, *brothers and sisters*, in view of God's mercy, to offer your bodies as a living sacrifice, holy and pleasing to God—this is your true and proper worship.

ROMANS 12:1, NIV

Finally, *brothers and sisters*, whatever is true, whatever is noble, whatever is right, whatever is pure, whatever is lovely, whatever is admirable—if anything is excellent or praiseworthy—think about such things.

PHILIPPIANS 4:8, NIV

*Brothers and sisters*, pray for us.

I THESSALONIANS 5:25, NIV

Consider it pure joy, *my brothers and sisters*, whenever you face trials of many kinds.

JAMES 1:2, NIV

Over and over in the letters that circulated to the churches of the first century, believers in Jesus directly addressed one another as "brothers and sisters." This term was chosen over *the only other option for direct address*, "beloved" (as you'll see in chapter 7), by a margin of almost three to one. But that's not all! The apostles also *described* other believers as "brothers and sisters" another 111 times, even when they weren't addressing them directly. Here are a few examples:

65

Therefore let us stop passing judgment on one another. Instead, make up your mind not to put any stumbling block or obstacle in the way of a *brother or sister.*

ROMANS 14:13, NIV

Therefore, if food causes *my brother or sister* to fall into sin, I will never ever eat meat again, so that I will not cause *my brother or sister* to fall.

1 CORINTHIANS 8:13, AUTHOR'S TRANSLATION

Suppose *a brother or a sister* is without clothes and daily food. If one of you says to them, "Go in peace; keep warm and well fed," but does nothing about their physical needs, what good is it?

JAMES 2:15-16, NIV

Between the 77 instances of direct address and the 111 instances of self-description we find in the New Testament outside the Gospels, we have evidence that believers were continually positioning themselves alongside other believers as a new family. The apostles who wrote these things believed that God had so reconfigured natural social bonds at the Cross that everyone in Christ now belonged to one another as members of one family. Recognizing this new reality God had created meant putting their words to work by repeatedly calling each other "brother" and "sister."

## BLOOD AND COVENANT

A fair-minded reader who accepts the observations I have just made might wonder if the early Christians had not simply adopted a Jewish way of speaking to each other. Most early Christians were Jews, after all. Could it be that they naturally called one another "brothers and sisters"?

It is a fact that Jews referred to one another as "brothers and sisters."[5] They believed their common bloodline *and* common covenant set them apart from the rest of the world. You could cut yourself off from your people by rejecting either of these things. Intermarriage was forbidden, and that protected the bloodline. Covenant faithfulness was baked into every aspect of daily life, from food preparation to Sabbath observance to who you married. Spurn these, and you could be cut off from your people. Blood and law comprised the backbone of community identity for the Jewish people, who traced their ancestry back to Abraham. In this respect, they naturally called one another "brothers and sisters."

If Christians had constituted themselves as a Jewish sect only, their use of "brothers and sisters" would have been unremarkable. That's not at all what happened though. They began to welcome Gentiles into their movement, and they began calling them "brothers and sisters" too. This was altogether new. This was the miracle of the gospel and the magic of words on full display. Thankfully, we have a front-row seat to the moment it happened!

Acts 15 recounts the time Paul, Barnabas, and Peter were

called before a council of church leaders in Jerusalem to testify about their ministry to Gentiles. They described how
they had seen Gentiles receive the Holy Spirit upon believing
in Jesus. Gentiles who had not converted to Judaism experienced the same phenomenon the Jewish followers of Jesus
had at Pentecost. God filled these nonobservant non-Jews
with his Holy Spirit in the same way he had the observant
Jewish believers. In doing so, God signified his acceptance of
the Gentiles based on faith in Jesus alone, without respect to
the law. Since God himself had welcomed Gentiles into his
family, what else were Jewish believers to do?

During the Council of Jerusalem recorded in Acts 15,
the leaders of the church weighed the testimonies of these
missionaries, along with the words of the prophets. They
wisely determined that it was not up to them to *let Gentiles
in* on the movement. God *had already* done that. Their part
was to keep the door of faith wide open without making it
hard for Gentiles to enter. Nonobservant non-Jews had been
saved through faith when they heard the gospel, and God was
dwelling in them by his Holy Spirit. They were as clearly a
part of the people of God as it was possible for a person to
be. To demand that these Gentiles become more Jewish to be
accepted in the community would be tantamount to taking
a stand against God.

So how do you articulate this kind of decision to the
churches? You do it with a bombshell of a salutation: "From
the apostles and elders, *your [Jewish] brothers, to the Gentile
brothers and sisters* in Antioch, Syria, and Cilicia, greetings!"

(Acts 15:23, NET). Just look at the language of the letter sent from the Jerusalem Council: Jewish believers in positions of authority addressed nonobservant, non-Jewish new converts as "brothers and sisters." Whatever followed from this opening salutation was a family letter. The gospel of reconciliation was being proclaimed in the register of relationship.

From this point forward, the teaching was clear, if sometimes contested: Family relationships within the church were to be reckoned based on faith in Jesus, not ethnicity or law. In some way, I guess we could say that blood and covenant were still the defining characteristics of this new community: It's simply that "blood" meant "Jesus' blood," and "covenant" meant "the new covenant." Because of their common faith in Jesus, believers understood themselves to be one family, one household. But what, exactly, did it mean to call someone a "brother" or "sister" in the ancient world?

## THE SIBLING IDEAL IN NEW TESTAMENT TIMES

I have one biological sister, and no one has ever asked her, "So, when did you and Norman become siblings?" That's not how the whole sibling thing works. You become a brother to your older sister by being born. It's not exactly a decision one of you reaches after negotiation. The only decision you get to make is whether you're going to be a good sibling.

I was not an exemplary younger brother. My older sister would never say that she didn't want me when I was a born. But there might have been times she didn't want me when

I got older. (She probably wouldn't say this either, but it's true.) When she was a senior in high school, taking Advanced Placement classes, dating a football player, and applying for college, I was smoking behind the cafeteria with my loser friends. Though my memory is bad, I cannot recall ever having a significant conversation with my sister in high school. We didn't fight a lot, but that's because we didn't talk a lot. The absence of conflict does not mean the presence of love. We did not have an ideal sibling relationship.

What is the ideal sibling relationship? What did it mean for the earliest generation of Christians to call each other "brothers and sisters"? In his book *The Ancient Church as Family,* New Testament professor Joseph Hellerman answers these questions.[6] At the core of the sibling ideal in the ancient Mediterranean world stand two related ideas: *solidarity* and *support*. When Christians called each other "brothers and sisters," this is what they had in mind.

### Solidarity

Solidarity involves standing with your brother or sister no matter how challenging the circumstances. Solidarity says, "I see myself *in you*. We *belong to each other*, come what may." In the modern West, we often think of the husband-wife bond as the strongest in the family. It was not so in the ancient Mediterranean world. There, the bond between siblings was the core bond of a stable society.[7] Violation of that bond represented deep, almost unthinkable, transgression. That's why the first story of the first family living east of Eden involved fratricide, not divorce. Cain killed Abel. Adam didn't walk away from Eve. This was the writer's way of saying the world devolved into chaos as soon as sin entered the world. If a brother can kill a brother, society has hit the skids.[8]

When a brother finds delight in the happiness his sister experiences, simply because they belong to each other, that's solidarity. When one sibling is weighed down by grief and the burden is experienced as a common possession, that's solidarity. If we are honest, this ancient ideal stands in stark contrast to our modern Western ideal. Today, siblings are expected to separate from one another and stand on their own two feet. If they call periodically and remember birthdays, they've discharged their duty as siblings. That is not exactly solidarity. The following verses, however, are:

I beg you, *brothers and sisters*, become like me, because I have become like you. . . . You know it was because of a physical illness that I first proclaimed the gospel to you, and though my physical condition put you to the test, you did not despise or reject me.

GALATIANS 4:12-14, NET

*Brotherly love* must continue. . . . Remember those in prison as though you were in prison with them, and those ill-treated as though you too felt their torment.

HEBREWS 13:1, 3, NET

It does not take keen imagination to see how a feeling of solidarity might translate into practical support for siblings. This is the second aspect of the sibling ideal in the ancient Mediterranean world.

## Support

Brothers and sisters were expected to translate their sense of mutual identification into tangible acts of material support when trouble came. In the ancient Mediterranean world, a stranger could be expected to look the other way if he saw you in distress, but "a brother is born for a time of adversity" (Proverbs 17:17, NIV). The drama of the Good Samaritan (Luke 10:30-37) really builds on this stage of expectation. When you are lying in a ditch, bleeding to death because you were waylaid while walking through treacherous territory, you expect your brothers and sisters to help you! You should also expect a stranger who is an ethnic enemy to pass you by. Strangers and enemies do that sort of thing, but your brothers and sisters stop to help. That's why the parable of the Good Samaritan is so powerful. In it Jesus was forecasting the kind of community he was creating. See how his followers John and James pick up this ideal of material support:

> This is how we know what love is: Jesus Christ laid
> down his life for us. And we ought to lay down
> our lives for *our brothers and sisters*. If anyone has
> material possessions and sees a brother or sister in

need but has no pity on them, how can the love of God be in that person?

I JOHN 3:16-17, NIV

What good is it, *my brothers and sisters*, if someone claims to have faith but has no deeds? Can such faith save them? Suppose a brother or a sister is without clothes and daily food. If one of you says to them, "Go in peace; keep warm and well fed," but does nothing about their physical needs, what good is it?

JAMES 2:14-16, NIV

Material support is the natural outgrowth of sibling solidarity. The authors of the New Testament believed God reconfigured our relationships along these lines because of the gospel. It's worth asking ourselves whether solidarity and support describe our relationships within and among our churches today.

# THE GOSPEL OF RECONCILIATION IN ONE WORD

We face a unique tension in the church today. People still call one another "brother" and "sister" at times, but these terms have lost a good bit of their organic unnaturalness. When we use the terms at all, we often use them as a sort of title. I grew up in a tradition where people called our pastor "Brother Rob." When my dad went to church with his biological brother, Danny, he called him "Brother Danny." If he had called him "Brother Danny" at the Thanksgiving table, it would have been incredibly weird. You only called people "Brother" when you were at church.

During the first three hundred years of the church, people didn't do this sort of thing. The phrase *brothers and sisters* was a description, not a title.[1] Peter once called Paul "our beloved brother Paul" (2 Peter 3:15), but this was an organically unnatural way for one Christian to describe another. About a hundred years later, one guy named Marcion was referred to as "our brother Marcion" in "The Martyrdom of Polycarp," one of the books in *The Apostolic Fathers*.[2] It seems obvious enough, however, that this reference was also organic, not conventional or titular.

I call the New Testament use of "brothers and sisters" organic because it wasn't a formal means of polite or respectful address. This didn't mean it felt natural, at least not at first. To the contrary, it probably felt as unnatural as any proclamation of the gospel feels: true to reality, but a little funny coming out of your mouth the first few times.

## CALLING ONE ANOTHER "BROTHERS AND SISTERS" . . . NATURALLY?

I would like us to get back to an organically unnatural use of *brother* and *sister* as terms of direct address and self-description in the church because I think it will shape Christian communities in a gospel-centered way. Calling one another the right thing—in this case, "brother" or "sister"—recognizes the work Jesus has already done and gives a certain shape to our relationships. Doing so won't *make* us brothers and sisters; God has already done that. Doing so will make a difference, however.

The challenge for many of us is that we can't conceive of a way to do this naturally. The answer to this challenge is quite simple: Do it unnaturally. You don't have to feel like family to acknowledge with your words that you *are*, in fact, one family in Christ. I am quite certain this challenge is as old as the church itself. I doubt the first generation of Jewish believers felt warm and fuzzy about calling Gentile believers their "brothers and sisters." (Some of them had probably grown up calling them "dogs.") It's simply not natural to begin openly identifying people you don't know or even like as your siblings. We can turn to the short book of Philemon as a case study in this tension and let this ancient letter guide us in a modern application.

Almost everything we can know about Philemon, a slave owner and Christian, and Onesimus, his slave, we discover from the one-page piece of correspondence Paul sent to Philemon. We know this letter was to be read in his house church in Colossae. If we could turn this piece of parchment into a brief, one-act stage drama, here's how the dramatis personae list would read at the beginning:

*Paul*.....................................letter writer; *brother* of
Philemon and Onesimus

*Philemon* ..............................recipient of letter;
*brother* of Paul and
Onesimus, his slave

*Onesimus*..............................letter bearer; *brother* of
Paul and Philemon,
his master

Anyone seeing this in the ancient Mediterranean world would immediately think, *That's absurd! A brother cannot be a slave to his own brother.* It would seem as socially perverse as a man marrying his own mother. (Sophocles already held the copyright to that drama.) Even so, this fictional dramatis personae captures an actual situation Paul was dealing with in his day.

Paul had led Philemon to Christ sometime in the past (Philemon 1:19). This made the two of them brothers (Philemon 1:7). Later, Paul led Philemon's slave, Onesimus, to faith in Christ (Philemon 1:10). This made all three of them brothers (Philemon 1:16). It also meant that Philemon now owned his brother as a slave. As if this weren't problematic enough, it seems that Onesimus had run away from Philemon (Philemon 1:17-18) and encountered Paul sometime during his flight. After leading him to faith in Christ, Paul was sending Onesimus back to Philemon so that his master could do the next right thing. (There is a possibility that Philemon sent Onesimus to Paul to mediate a dispute between master and slave. Even if this is the case, there was tension in a relationship with an immense power differential.) This return journey must have been a very difficult choice for Onesimus to make. Depending on the circumstances under which he had left, his master might have possessed the legal power of life and death over him according to Roman law.

There is no chance that Onesimus and Philemon "felt like family" to one another at this point in their personal histories. They were not brothers with warm, affectionate feelings. They were brothers because they had each been "born again" (John 3:3) into the same family because of the heavenly Father's love for them in Christ. They were related to one another with a bond that transcended and reconfigured their past relationship as master and slave.

To make this reality painfully obvious, Paul said to Philemon: "Perhaps it was for this reason that [Onesimus] was separated from you for a little while, so that you would have him back eternally, no longer as a slave, but more than a slave, *as a dear brother.* He is especially so to me, and even more so to you now, both humanly speaking and in the Lord" (Philemon 1:15-16, NET). Paul believed that the polarity of their past relationship, any enmity that had pushed them apart, had been reversed "in the Lord." Whatever wrongs these two men had done to one another, whatever the power differential between them, they were now brothers in Christ.

For Paul, there was an obvious next step for Philemon to make: The first and most basic thing for Philemon to do involved recognizing Onesimus as his brother in the same way that Paul was. If Philemon did so, all the expectations of solidarity and support among siblings (see the previous chapter) would kick in. He would have to face the fact that he now owned his brother as a slave and would hopefully feel the social perversity of this.

I think Paul's method of negotiating this tension is wise, if not genius. He did not *tell Philemon what to do*, but he did make it clear *who Onesimus was* to Philemon. He sent Onesimus back to Philemon as if to say, "Now, here is your brother. What are you going to do with him?" Would Philemon relate to Onesimus with the expected solidarity? Would he forgive Onesimus whatever wrongs he had done and receive him as a brother should? (Onesimus would have had to do the same thing, and I imagine Paul helped him accept this.) I do not think it is an overstatement to say that the entire drama of Philemon turns on the word *brother*.[3]

## SAY IT LIKE IT IS . . . AND SHAPE SOLIDARITY

What I want you to take away from Paul's letter to Philemon is that *there was nothing natural about a slave calling his master "brother"* or vice versa. Identifying someone as a "brother" or "sister" in Christ names a fact, not a feeling.

You don't have to wait to conjure up feelings of solidarity to call someone a "brother" or "sister." After all, do you always feel warm affection when you call your biological siblings "brother" or "sister"? In modern times, this rarely functions as a term of endearment. More often, it's simply a statement of fact. It *may* bring positive feelings with it, but that's not a prerequisite or even a necessary outcome. The more important thing is that we use the terms *brother* and *sister* to identify the relationship God has created and affirm the commitment that is consistent with those words.

When my first wife passed away, my sister called to ask me an unexpected question: Would I like one of her daughters to move from Alabama to Wisconsin to help around the house for a while? My sister knew that I was completely incapable of managing a household with kids at home. I cannot cook, I buy groceries impulsively, and money only interests me at the theoretical level. I wear the same clothes multiple days in a row, forget birthdays, and never remember to repay money I have borrowed. My sister knew I needed help, and she was willing to volunteer one of my nieces as tribute. (I can only suppose my nieces knew about this arrangement and were willing participants.) Though I didn't take her up on the offer, it was one of the most sisterly things a sibling could do.

If you recall from the previous chapter, my sister and I do not share the closest of relationships. We love each other, but we live half a continent away too. We share parents and occasional holidays together, and that is about all. Even so, when my wife died, my sister clearly believed she had a responsibility to me *as a sister* that no one else in the world had. Though she is kind, she was not simply being kind—she was being *a sister*. She was showing the kind of solidarity and support appropriate for siblings. Siblings do for one another what no one else is expected to do.

That's how it is supposed to be in the church today, and that's why it is imperative for us to begin recognizing the believers around us (and around the world) as our brothers and sisters. Saying it like it is will shape our expressions of solidarity and support because it is hard to look someone in the eye, call them "brother," and then treat them like they don't exist. Your brother cannot be your enemy unless you live in the Marvel Comics universe and your brother is Loki.

Even then, you will have to work out the complex dynamics of being a sibling to a person who is trying to destroy you.

There's a good chance that your Christian brothers and sisters are not trying to destroy you, even though you may be separated by a wide gap of wealth, race, politics, and theology. If they are doing things that tear you down or wear you down, they are being lousy brothers and sisters, I suppose. But being a bad sibling does not mean you have become a not-sibling, nor does having a bad sibling confer on you permission to treat them the same way. Learning how to address and describe these believers around you as "brothers and sisters" may even be critical to repairing relationships and shaping communities in a gospel-centered way. There is enough tribalism in the modern world to keep us separated. But the Cross of Christ has already closed the gaps between us. Our job is simply to see it like it is, say it like it is, and live accordingly.

This is what it looks like in my world today:

- Brianna is a young Black woman who helps lead a campus group I oversee in Minneapolis. After our student group studied Mark 3 a few months back (the passage where Jesus identifies his followers as "brothers and sisters"), I started calling her "my little sister." Now she calls me "Uncle Norman."

- Carson is an ex-convict who attends a Christian support group I visit occasionally.[4] He was the first person to introduce himself to me when I went the first time. Since then, I reintroduce myself to him by saying, "Carson, my brother. Good to see you." I'm never sure he remembers who I am, but he usually responds positively when I call him "brother."

• Sergei and his family fled Russia after his country invaded Ukraine. They waited at the US-Mexico border for two months, seeking asylum in the United States. I prayed for them to gain entrance into the country during that time. When they finally made it to our city, I met him at a conference and said, "So you are the brother I've been praying for. Welcome!"[5]

Notice that I didn't call these people "Brother Sergei" or "Sister Brianna." You can do that if it works in your world. But I would also urge you to think beyond the conventional use of these words as titles and try to find a more common way to identify people as your Christian siblings. Often I do this by starting a sentence with something like "You are my brother/sister, and . . . ." This does not necessarily feel natural. It doesn't have to. Just say it like it is.

It may be tempting to say to yourself at this point, *I think it may be enough if I just* think about *other Christians as my siblings*. I want you to be careful about this kind of reasoning though. Calling people "brothers and sisters" is a proclamation of the gospel, not a nice thing to think about. The gospel did not transform communities in the first centuries after Christ because people thought about it everywhere they went. They openly talked about the gospel. Calling one another "brothers and sisters" was one of the clearest, easiest ways to do so, and it can be again.

Leave it up to God to give us such a simple way to express a reality only he could create. Sometimes, you will be identifying people as your siblings across gaps that seem impossible to cross. Just remember, God has already bridged that gap with the Cross. The historical forces that have separated you are not greater than the Savior who has reconciled you.

## SAY WHAT YOU MEAN AND MEAN WHAT YOU SAY

We all know that it's possible to say one thing and live contrary to it. You could call someone your "sister" and then live like she has no claim on you. We have a word for this kind of thing: *hypocrisy*. When we see it, we hate it. When we see it in ourselves, we *really* hate it (though it's harder to see it in ourselves). This is one argument for beginning to call all Christians in your world "brothers and sisters" as often as possible. We will not be able to withstand our own consciences if we do so and then turn our backs on these people when it matters most.

We cannot say to a Russian Christian, "You are my brother," and subsequently treat him like a stranger with no claim on us. We certainly cannot call him a brother and regard him as an enemy because the dictator who runs his country invaded Ukraine. International politics does not supersede family relationships. We cannot say "You are my sister" to a believer and then disparage her convictions on egalitarian or complementarian theology, as though she were an enemy of the church. We cannot call an ex-convict "brother" and hold him at an arm's distance because he has lots of tattoos or little money.

Of course, calling other believers "brother" or "sister" doesn't mean you have to agree with the political or theological convictions they hold. Siblings in nuclear or blended families disagree with each another, in case you haven't noticed. It's no different in the church.

Our differences don't disappear because Jesus brought us together. He doesn't flatten our cultural preferences or ask us to surrender our convictions. Jesus is not the great leveler of ethnic distinctions or personal preferences. The more Christians you put in the room and the longer they stay there, the more their differences will become apparent. This doesn't make them not-a-family. Siblings simply know that family bonds matter more than family disagreements. Underneath all their turbulence there is relationship that makes it possible for them to love and support one another without agreeing on everything.

I love my sister and her family, but I do not want to move in with her. She would certainly say the same thing about me. Even so, our relationship is never in question, and we have proven it time after time. In the same way, you can love your brothers and sisters in Christ without wanting to join their church or support their social cause. If you are an egalitarian, you don't have to go to a complementarian church just to prove that you regard them as your family. If you are a Pentecostal believer, the life will get sucked out of you if you join a church that doesn't allow expressive worship. You don't have to move into your brother or sister's house to prove that you are in the same family. You simply have to accept that you are, now, one family in Christ and follow the logical steps toward solidarity and support.

## WHAT IT MEANS TO BE SIBLINGS

One of my best friends from college, Jeff, baptizes babies. He doesn't do this randomly on the streets of Tuscaloosa, Alabama, where he lives. Rather, he pastors a Presbyterian church, and baptizing babies is one of the things you do in that tradition. I hold a different view on baptizing infants. I could argue the point with my friend Jeff, and he could argue back. Both of us are seminary trained, and both of us have attended churches that practice the mode of baptism we *do not* endorse. We are familiar with the contours of the debate. On a recent backpacking trip, however, Jeff and I spent a grand total of *zero minutes* discussing this difference.

Jeff already knows my reasons for baptizing people only after they've trusted in Christ personally, and I know his reasons for baptizing babies as a sign of their inclusion in the covenant community of Christ. On the right night around the right campfire, we might even enjoy arguing about the merits of our respective positions. For the two nights we were in Oak Mountain State Park near Birmingham, Alabama, though, we didn't bring them up. We simply walked beside lakes, scanned the trail ahead of us, and tried to keep up with our wives. Mostly, we just enjoyed being together. We laughed about our eccentricities, shared our losses, and told stories about our time in college. We ate granola bars, helped one another set up camp, and complained about how hard it is to sleep on the ground after you turn fifty. When we made it back to our cars after two nights on the trail, we would have gladly gone on for two more, because it is "good and . . . pleasant . . . for brothers to dwell together in unity" (Psalm 133:1). This is the same kind of love I want to show for other Christians I didn't meet in college, a kind of love that doesn't ignore differences but doesn't exaggerate them unnecessarily.

For Jeff and me, the theological gap between us is beggared by the love that saved us and brought us into relationship as brothers. It might even be fair to say that we have chosen to magnify our common Savior instead of our different theologies *because* we are brothers. The physical distance between us keeps us from having to confront these differences very often. However, I'm pretty sure Jeff would be my pastor if I were ever forced to move to Tuscaloosa, Alabama. (God forbid. I am an Auburn graduate.) Even if he weren't, he would still be my brother.

You can act like you don't have a big, strange family, but other believers will still be your brothers and sisters. You won't become any less related to them by acting like they have no part in your life. You didn't choose them, and they didn't choose you. But here you are because God is God. Now how will you respond?

Cordoning yourself off from Christians who aren't like you or who don't like you doesn't turn them into non–family members. It just makes you a bad brother or sister, and it distorts the gospel. Because God has exercised his power to make peace with all of us at the Cross, our baked-in prejudices, preferences, and proper convictions do not provide us with a warrant for wall building within the Kingdom of God.

Every time you call another believer your "brother" or "sister," you make this clear. You proclaim the gospel to your siblings, to the world, and, most importantly, to yourself. When you do so across cultural gaps, the proclamation gets louder in a fractured world. You don't need six syllables (rec-on-cil-i-a-tion) or a half-hour sermon with a PowerPoint to explain what Jesus did at the Cross. Just two syllables—"sister" or "broth-er"—will do. Simple words, deliberately used, change everything—because the gospel is the power of God for salvation.

# BELOVED

*What We Called Our Enemies
and the Other Strangers God Saved*

In the early church, brothers and sisters in Christ called each other more than just "brothers and sisters in Christ." They may have used that term more than any other, but they did not use it exclusively. In fact, Paul often paired the word *brother* with the word *beloved*. This is, in fact, the way Paul referred to Onesimus, the slave, and his master, Philemon, in the New Testament letters of Colossians and Philemon. These two letters were almost certainly sent at the same time to the same community.[1] In fact, both would have probably been read *aloud* within the house church Philemon belonged to. We sometimes think of the letter Paul wrote to Philemon as private correspondence because it was a personal appeal.

It was certainly not meant as a private letter, however. Paul makes it clear in his greeting that he intends the letter to be read to "the church [that meets] in your house" (Philemon 1:2). That means everyone, including Onesimus, would have heard Paul use the following descriptions of Philemon, the master, and his slave, Onesimus:

> Paul, a prisoner of Christ Jesus, and Timothy our brother, to *Philemon, our beloved* and our fellow worker . . .
>
> PHILEMON 1:1, AUTHOR'S TRANSLATION[2]

> Perhaps [Onesimus] was for this reason separated from you for a while, that you would have him back forever, no longer as a slave, but more than a slave, *a beloved brother*, especially to me, but how much more to you, both in the flesh and in the Lord.
>
> PHILEMON 1:15-16

Paul didn't simply regard these two men as brothers. He also reintroduced them to one another as "beloved." Apart from the term *brothers and sisters*, the word translated above as "beloved" (Greek *agapētos*) is *the only other customary form of direct address* in the New Testament outside the Gospels and Acts. By the numbers, *beloved* is used twenty-nine times in direct address and twenty-three times in self-description. Almost all the writers of the New Testament letters used the term *beloved*. Even Jude called his audience "beloved" three times on the one page of parchment he contributed to the canon of Scripture.

## THE GRAMMAR OF *LOVE*

On a technical level, the Greek word translated "beloved" is an adjective that functions normally by modifying a noun. When Paul called Onesimus a "beloved brother" (Colossians 4:9; Philemon 1:16), the word was functioning normally. You might remember from your school days, however, that adjectives can sometimes stand on their own, taking the place of nouns. When they do this, they draw attention to themselves. In short, they take a descriptive attribute and stand it up in the discourse like it's a thing itself. (An adjective standing in place of a noun is usually called a *substantive adjective*.)

You don't just find this sort of thing in classrooms or Greek manuscripts. It's a common feature of language. Did you ever see the old Clint Eastwood movie *The Good, the Bad, and the Ugly*? The title would not have been as snappy if it was *The Good People, the Bad People, and the Ugly People*. Victor Hugo's famous novel *Les Misérables* ("*The Wretched*") would have sounded a little less dramatic if he had titled it *Les Gens Misérables* ("*The Wretched People*"). When we talk about caring for "the elderly," it would be cumbersome to say "the elderly people." You see what I mean? There's a punchiness to our descriptions when adjectives stand on their own like nouns. They draw attention to the characteristic we want our audience to focus on.

Take another example. If I introduced my wife to you as "Kristy, the beautiful,"[3] and then kept on referring to her throughout our conversation as "the beautiful," you would take note. You might find it charming initially, or you might find it weird immediately. Either way, you wouldn't be able to avoid it. In a similar way, calling *people* who are poor "the poor" takes one characteristic of their lives and magnifies it in a discourse. This might be done to relegate them to the sidelines ("Well, of course *the poor* would vote for raising minimum wage") or it might be done to elevate their status ("Surely *the poor* know best what constitutes a livable wage"). You can only know why this attribute is being magnified by paying attention to the context. The point is not that adjectives acting like nouns are good or bad (or ugly). They are simply one effective way for a speaker to draw attention to a characteristic so outstanding that it takes on a life of its own. In the New Testament, one such characteristic is *beloved*. Believers are so loved that being loved becomes an identity marker. It defines who they are. This raises an immediate question: *Loved by whom?*

## "BELOVED" BY WHOM?

When the writers of the New Testament called people "beloved," did they mean "you who are loved by God" or "you who are loved by me/us (the writer/community)"? All these are possibilities, and the context usually makes it clear. For instance, when Paul begins his letter to the churches in Rome, he addresses it "to all who are *beloved of God* in Rome, called as saints" (Romans 1:7). It is very clear that Paul meant to say, "You, Romans, are loved by God." When he ends the letter to the Romans, however, he greets several people by name and calls some of them "beloved." He says, for instance, "Greet Ampliatus, *my beloved in the Lord*" (Romans 16:8). Notice that he does not say that Ampliatus is beloved *by* the Lord, though this was certainly true. Rather, the author meant that he (Paul) loved Ampliatus *in* the Lord. Their relationship in Christ meant they stood in relationship to one another as "beloved." When you see the word *beloved* in the New Testament, this is the typical way it is being used.[4] We are "beloved" within Christian community by our fellow believers.

What a proclamation of the gospel! All who have experienced the reconciling love of God in Christ have been reconciled to one another as well. Those who were formerly estranged have been brought into loving communion with one another because of the death and resurrection of Jesus. These changes in identity and social relations did not develop over time because of a concentrated effort on our part; rather, they changed in an instant at the Cross. We became "beloved" the same way we became "brothers and sisters"—by believing in Jesus Christ. The gospel changes everything, including our fundamental identities in the sight of God and his people.

This does not mean, of course, that we feel loving affection toward everyone who is "beloved." We cannot say about every Christian what Paul said of the Philippians: "God is my witness, how I *long for* you all with the *affection* of Christ Jesus" (Philippians 1:8). *Longing* and *affection* are indications of deep love, but they are not synonyms for it. Calling someone your "beloved in Christ" is a statement about who they are, not how you feel. Loving someone is not the same thing as feeling close to them, though the latter may come the longer we choose love. Loving has far more in common with choosing than feeling.

There was no other way for Philemon and Onesimus to understand Paul's words to them than this explanation. There was very little chance the master and runaway slave felt affection toward one another. Their relationship had been defined by wrongdoing and tension embedded in a system of human oppression, yet Paul expected them to receive and relate to one another as "beloved." It cannot be supposed that Paul was commanding them *to feel* a certain way. Rather, he was asking them to acknowledge a fundamental shift in their relationship that had happened when each had received Christ. Because God had chosen them, Paul could call both men "beloved" with the expectation they would make a choice for one another.

It's worth noting that being beloved does not mean being friends. Paul was not commanding Onesimus and Philemon to foster a friendship. Friendship grows through a long process of trust building, open communication, and shared experience. You don't become someone's "beloved" in Christ this way. Loving and trust-filled friendships are earned, sustained, and lost on the natural plane of human relations. Being "beloved" within the Christian community is a grace gift conferred by God on all who are in Christ. Friendship and affection may arise within the community of those who are "beloved," but friendship and affection do not create it. The Cross has done that already.

This is why I do not love the way some English versions of the Bible translate the word *beloved* (Greek *agapētos*) as "dear friends." I certainly understand the attempt to render the Greek into normal-sounding English. Frankly, "dear friends" sounds much more normal than "beloved."[5] Most people only associate the word *beloved* with weddings or Prince's song "Let's Go Crazy" ("Dearly beloved, we are gathered here today . . .").[6] So it seems reasonable that translators would prefer a more normal-sounding phrase like *dear friends*. The problem with this translation is that friendship is a status we earn, not a grace gift. Adding the word *dear* only compounds the problem. The average person would probably say they have no more than a handful of people they count as "dear friends." This is *precisely the opposite meaning* of the Greek term *agapētos* as it is used in the New Testament. The word *beloved* isn't beset with the same problem (perhaps because no one uses it normally anyway).

Your "beloved" is not your spouse or that unique friend who shares almost everything with you. Your "beloved" are those who have Christ in common with you, even if you share nothing else. Because God chose you, you are "beloved" to one another. Because God chose you, you choose to love. If you call someone "beloved" today, you will raise some eyebrows. It may or may not comfort you to know that this was undoubtedly true in the first-century church as well. As we will see in the next section, there is simply no evidence that people called one another "beloved" until the church began regularly referring to one another this way.

## THE RISE OF THE "BELOVED"

If you exclude the sensual and sacred poetry of Song of Solomon, the word *beloved* (or its equivalents) doesn't appear all that often in the Old Testament. This is significant because the earliest Christians sourced a lot of their vocabulary from the Old Testament. These are the only times where some form of the word *beloved* is used in the Old Testament to describe the people of God:

- "Of Benjamin he said, 'May *the beloved of the LORD* dwell in security by Him, / Who shields him all the day, / And he dwells between His shoulders'" (Deuteronomy 33:12).

- "Save us and help us with your right hand, / that *those you love* may be delivered" (Psalm 60:5, NIV, repeated verbatim in Psalm 108:6).

- "Unless the LORD builds the house, / They labor in vain who build it; / Unless the LORD guards the city, / The watchman keeps awake in vain. / It is vain for you to rise up early, / To retire late, / To eat the bread of painful labors; / For He gives *to His beloved* even in his sleep" (Psalm 127:1-2).

- "I have forsaken My house, / I have abandoned My inheritance; / I have given *the beloved of My soul* / Into the hand of her enemies" (Jeremiah 12:7).

These verses are the only four examples in the Old Testament where the people of God are described as "beloved" or "loved ones." There are many, many places in the Old Testament where God says he loves his people and even commands them to love one another. But the term *beloved* is simply not used as an identity marker for the people of God in the Old Testament. So we must conclude that Christians didn't adopt this form of self-description from the Jewish Scriptures. (There is an alternative, of course. People all around them—Jews, Greeks, and Romans—could have called one another "beloved" all the time. This does not appear to be the case either though.)

When people in the wider Greco-Roman world of the first century used the term *beloved*, they almost always used it in reference to children—often an only son—or affectionately regarded acquaintances. You can see examples of this usage in the New Testament. At his baptism, Jesus was identified by a voice from heaven as God's "beloved Son" (Matthew 3:17; see also Jesus' transfiguration in Matthew 17:5). Paul also identified several affectionately regarded individuals as "beloved." For instance, he closes his letter to the Romans by saying, "Greet Epaenetus, *my beloved*, who is the first convert to Christ from Asia" (Romans 16:5). Evidence suggests that lots of people used the term *beloved* in this way in the first century. But they were always referring to individuals who stood in some special relationship to them. No one said things like this:

- "Those who have believers as their masters must not be disrespectful to them because they are brethren, but must serve them all the more, because those who partake of the benefit are believers and *beloved*. Teach and preach these principles" (1 Timothy 6:2).

- "*Beloved*, if God so loved us, we also ought to love one another" (1 John 4:11).

Calling groups of people—many of whom you didn't regard as dear friends—"beloved" would have been remarkable in the first century. Asking Christian slaves to regard their Christian masters as "beloved" (1 Timothy 6:2) would have sounded as preposterous then as it does today.

So what explains the rise of "beloved" as the second-most-common form of direct address and self-description in early church discourse? It seems that this term developed at the same time and in the same way as the Greek word *agapē*.

There is no question that *agapē*, "love," was the primary

term early Christians used to describe the love God had demonstrated for them in Christ:

> God demonstrates His own love [*agapē*] toward us,
> in that while we were yet sinners, Christ died for us.
> ROMANS 5:8

> Now these three remain: faith, hope, and love. But
> the greatest of these is love [*agapē*].
> I CORINTHIANS 13:13, NET

> God is love [*agapē*].
> I JOHN 4:8

In the first century, *agapē* would have been an unusual noun to use to describe God's disposition toward and choice of unworthy sinners. As a noun, *agapē* simply wasn't used in Greco-Roman discourse.[7] It does appear fifteen times in the Greek translation of the Old Testament (the Septuagint), but ten of these are in the sensual love poem Song of Solomon. When you contrast that with the *116 times* the noun appears in the Greek New Testament, you begin to understand just how prominent the term became in the early Christian era. It would not be an overstatement to say that the term *agapē* experienced a meteoric rise in the New Testament. It became the dominant term Christians used to describe the kind of relationship God had with those in Christ. Therefore, it is not surprising that it became the dominant term Christians used to describe the kind of relationship they had with *one another* in Christ.

Notice how John correlates the *agapē* love of God for his people and their own relationship as a community of the "beloved":

> Beloved, let us love one another, for love is from God; and everyone who loves is born of God and knows God. The one who does not love does not know God, for God is love. By this the love of God was manifested in us, that God has sent His only begotten Son into the world so that we might live through Him. In this is love, not that we loved God, but that He loved us and sent His Son to be the propitiation for our sins. Beloved, if God so loved us, we also ought to love one another.
>
> 1 JOHN 4:7-11

The love we show to one another in the community of the "beloved" should be like the love we receive from God. It does not move along the well-worn grooves of reciprocal kindness. That's friendship. It doesn't require personal chemistry, like romantic love. It doesn't seek out a worthy recipient. If God had loved us this way, we would all be damned.

God chose us in Christ. This is the closest synonym we have to describe God's love for us. "*Agapē* is not a sentimental feeling," wrote biblical scholar Ceslaus Spicq in his magnum opus on *agapē* in the New Testament, "but the intention of doing good . . . a profound desire searching for means of expression."[8] The best way I know to represent the outworking of this extraordinary love of God among the "beloved" is to put the word into a funnel.

## WHERE DO YOUR "BELOVED" BELONG?

Think about the relational dynamics you have experienced as your relationships with people have grown over time. The progression usually goes something like this:

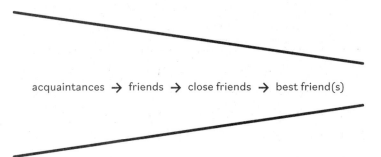

acquaintances → friends → close friends → best friend(s)

Obviously, you have more acquaintances and friends than you do close friends. The question is *On which side of this diagram would you put someone who is your "beloved"?* Most people would unhesitatingly put a "beloved" person on the far right, far beyond "acquaintances" and maybe beyond a "best friend." In natural human community, you become "beloved" through unique chemistry and commitment.

In supernatural human community—that is, in the church—you become "beloved" when God saves you by grace through faith in Christ. You begin the journey of Christian relationship with love.

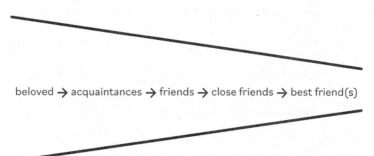

beloved → acquaintances → friends → close friends → best friend(s)

Within the church, you are "beloved" by people with whom you have nothing in common except Jesus. Love is your starting point within the community. Every believer you encounter and millions you will only meet in the world to come are your "beloved." This is not a statement of aspiration, chemistry, or deep feeling. It's just a reality. It is the gospel of reconciliation in a word.

## BEGIN WITH LOVE

The gospel of reconciliation invites us to begin with love in every encounter with a brother or sister. Most of us are familiar with the Golden Rule: "In everything, do to others what you would have them do to you" (Matthew 7:12, NIV). Based on everything we've learned so far, we could modify this teaching and say: "Do for others *what God has done for you.*" This is what John counseled the community of the "beloved" in the passage I quoted on page 100. Because it's so important, I will repeat it here with special emphasis:

> Beloved, let us love one another, *for* love is from God; and everyone who loves is born of God and knows God. The one who does not love does not know God, *for* God is love. By this the love of God was manifested in us, *that* God has sent His only begotten Son into the world *so that* we might live through Him. In this is love, *not that* we loved God, *but that* He loved us and sent His Son to be the propitiation for our sins. Beloved, *if* God so loved us, [then] we also ought to love one another.
>
> I JOHN 4:7-11

I once heard a teacher say that you can map the logic of almost any passage in the Bible by highlighting the words that connect the clauses. I've italicized John's logic in the passage above to focus your attention on one undeniable fact: Those who know the love of God in Christ show the love of God to all who are in Christ. They love as they have been loved. This means that we begin with love, since that is how God began with us.

Beginning with love will mean loving people we don't like. Christians are to love—and can love!—those they do not agree with or feel affinity for. They can love people they barely know, knowing God has loved them in Christ, just as they are. After all, God did not "like" us when we were his enemies; he loved us. He did not probe our responsiveness to his overtures of kindness to see if we would reciprocate. He didn't wait to see if we would prove ourselves worthy of his attention. He certainly didn't look for people with whom he had personal chemistry. Rather, he created the world, watched it fall, and began his redeeming work . . . all with a disposition to love us. *God is love.* He did not end with love at the Cross after generations of judgment. He began with love at Creation, and our personal relationship with him is a testament to this.

When police killed George Floyd in Minneapolis on May 25, 2020, the city erupted in violent protest for days. My wife and I live in suburban Saint Paul, Minnesota, about fifteen miles from the epicenter of the rioting. Downtown Minneapolis does not exactly feel like home to us, but the events shaking the city shook us, too. When things settled down a bit, we started exploring ways to get more involved with people who were trying to rebuild the community. In June of that year, we drove to worship at Nu Way Missionary Baptist Church, a historically Black church in downtown Minneapolis.

Looking back, I cannot say whether we made a good decision. The events of May 25 had sparked worldwide protests, and racial tensions were at an all-time high across the city. I'm not sure that Nu Way needed a white couple with four kids to show up on their doorstep that day. That's what happens when you are a church, however: People you do not know show up on your doorstep.

The day our family attended, fifteen concrete steps promised to keep us out of the building. Our daughter, Lauren, was in a wheelchair, and there was no accessible entrance to the sanctuary. The only way in was up. As we stood there, unsure of what to do next, an usher descended the steps. After a moment of discussion, he said, "Let me help you carry her in."

I can stand outside this memory and watch the scene unfold. I see a young Black man helping carry my daughter into church on a day when we probably shouldn't have been there. I do not know how he felt, but he showed me how he loved. This is the gospel of reconciliation.

# SAINTS

*What We Called the Ordinary People*
*Who Surrounded Us in the Dark*

If the self-designation *beloved* (from the previous chapter) is a word we see and hear very seldom, the word *saint* is one I see every day. I do live in Saint Paul, Minnesota, after all. There's a pretty good chance that many of you see or hear the word *saint* a time or two each week also. We name our towns, colleges, and cathedrals after saints. We watch NFL football and see the New Orleans Saints play. We come across movies or TV series with the word *saints* in the title. In many regions of the world, it's simply not an option to get away from the "saints." And by the end of this chapter, I hope you won't want to.

You should know up front that we are using the word *saint*

today in a way that sharply departs from the way it was used in the New Testament. The word has taken on connotations that it never had when our faith was young, and the changes approach distortion. Words, of course, naturally shift their meanings over time. Sometimes the shifts are almost bizarre, but most are relatively neutral. I remember trying to explain to my grandmother in the 1980s how the word *bad* meant "good" to my friends. (She concluded we were all just petulant children.)

But in this case, using the word *saints* to mean what it *didn't* mean in the New Testament is not a neutral change in definition. Like the other words we have examined in this book, *saints* is a gospel word that tells us about the fundamental way our relationship to God and one another has changed at the Cross. If we come across this word in our Bibles and assume it means the opposite of its true definition, we stand on very poor footing. What is more, we are less likely to use this word if we misunderstand it. This puts us at risk of muting the gospel in our conversations.

## THE DEFINITION OF A MISTAKE

If you compound the various meanings given for the word *saint* in *Merriam-Webster's Collegiate Dictionary* (eleventh edition), you come away with a picture of someone who is "preeminent for holiness," "eminent for piety or virtue," or "illustrious."[1] Though most people do not use language this lofty in their everyday speech, this compounded definition captures what comes into most people's minds when they hear the word *saints*.

And it is wrong.

So far as New Testament teaching goes, modern people are missing (and misrepresenting) the meaning of *saint*. Two observations should drive this point home. First, notice that no one called anyone else "Saint So-and-So" in the New Testament. I live near the "Church of St. Peter," just north of the city of "Saint Paul," not too far from the "Basilica of Saint Mary." No one called Peter, Paul, or Mary "Saint" when they were alive. As far as the written record is concerned, no one called anyone else "Saint" (with a capital *S*) for several hundred years of the church's history. This doesn't mean it's wrong to do so today, but we should be very careful not to project this late use of "Saint" backward into the Bible.

We have good reason for this caution, also, when we make a second observation: The word *saints* (Greek *hagios*) was almost never used in the New Testament as a singular noun. In fact, of the sixty times the word is used—from Acts to Revelation—in reference to Christians, fifty-nine of them are plural.[2] In the only instance of the word being used in the singular, it still has a plural feel to it:

> Greet *every saint* [singular] in Christ Jesus. The brothers who are with me greet you. *All the saints* [plural] greet you, especially those who are of Caesar's household.
>
> PHILIPPIANS 4:21-22, AUTHOR'S TRANSLATION

The evidence of this plural usage on the pages of the New Testament is so overwhelming, it may not be an over-statement to say: In the early church, no *one* was a saint. We *all* were. "Saint" was not used to refer to a given eminent individual—or to any individual, for that matter. Christians regarded themselves as "saints" in the aggregate, as a community. But what did this mean to them?

### "SAINTLY" PEOPLE AND THINGS IN THE OLD TESTAMENT

The earliest generation of believers drew on the ideas and words of the Old Testament to express their beliefs about Jesus. This made sense because the earliest gospel proclamations were made to Jewish people. These early Christians did not believe Jesus had come to start a new religion. They believed the gospel announced the fulfillment of Old Testament patterns and prophecies. They saw far more continuity between the teachings of the Old Testament and the preaching of the gospel than many of us see today. For our purposes in this chapter, we will simply note that the early church didn't come up with the idea of being a "saint." They borrowed it from the Old Testament, and they invested it with a new dimension of meaning in light of the gospel.

It is fascinating to see what things are described as holy in the Old Testament. (Our English words *holy* and *saint* come from the same Greek root word.) The Temple at Jerusalem was holy, as was the hill on which the Temple sat. In fact, the city of

Jerusalem was holy, as were dates on the calendar (we still call them *holi*-days!). Bronze buckets were holy, along with anointing oil, wooden tent pegs, and specific body parts of animals offered as sacrifices. Did I mention the buckets (Exodus 38:3; 40:9-10)? What is it that each of these things has in common? Trust me when I say it was not their moral excellence. Rather, each had been taken out of common circulation and dedicated to God for use in worship. Because a certain hill in Jerusalem had been set apart for the Temple, no enterprising developer could rezone it to build apartments. Because certain bronze shovels and wooden tent pegs had been designated for use in the Tabernacle, they couldn't be sold at Home Depot for common use. It's not that they were exemplary shovels and pegs. They were not more ornate or durable than other shovels and pegs. They were simply the pegs and shovels that had been removed from common circulation for special use in the Tabernacle or Temple. No worker could pilfer a few pegs to use for a deck remodel at home. No priest could raffle off a few shovels to raise money for new carpet in the Temple. They were "holy"—we could equally say "saintly"—and were to be used exclusively in the Tabernacle or Temple. No moral evaluation is implicit in the use of the term.

Consider how this concept influences your understanding of the Sabbath day. In the Old Testament, the seventh day was "holy." What did this mean? Notice the way God commanded a Sabbath rest by emphasizing the way this day was to be taken out of common circulation:

"Remember the sabbath day, to keep it holy. *Six days you shall labor and do all your work*, but the seventh day is a sabbath of the LORD your God; in it you shall not do any work, you or your son or your daughter, your male or your female servant or your cattle or your sojourner who stays with you. For in six days the LORD made the heavens and the earth, the sea and all that is in them, and rested on the seventh day; therefore the LORD blessed the sabbath day and *made it holy*."

EXODUS 20:8-11

The seventh day was not "holy" (or "saintly") because it had inherent virtue. It was distinguished because God set it aside from the other six. The other six days were common days, where people were free to "labor and do all [their] work." Not so the seventh. God made the sabbath holy, a day reserved for his purposes to bless his people. This is a core component of "holiness" in the Old Testament,[3] and it also explains why Israel regarded themselves as a holy people.

God set Israel apart from the nations as his own. They were not intrinsically better behaved or more praiseworthy than any of the nations around them. They did not possess more virtue, wisdom, or strength such that God was drawn to them. They did not stand out. Rather they were set apart, chosen, and blessed.[4]

Lest they miss this point, Moses clarified it for them twice before they entered the Promised Land:

"You are a holy people to the LORD your God; the LORD your God has chosen you to be a people for His own possession out of all the peoples who are on the face of the earth.

"The LORD did not set His love on you nor choose you because you were more in number than any of the peoples, for you were the fewest of all peoples."

DEUTERONOMY 7:6-7

Moses punctuated the point later by saying, "Know, then, it is not because of your righteousness that the LORD your God is giving you this good land to possess, for you are a stubborn people" (Deuteronomy 9:6).

This was not a flattering thing to say to Israel, but it's an important observation for us to make: Israel's holiness was not synonymous with their intrinsic virtue or moral excellence. It described their relationship to God (and, thus, to one another) as the people he had set apart for his purposes.

This is what early church leaders meant to communicate when they borrowed the term from the Old Testament. The writers of the New Testament did not call Christians "holy" or "saints" because they were virtuous but because they were chosen. They believed that virtue flowed out of holiness, not the other way around. You became a better person because God had placed you among the saints. You did not become a "saint" because you were better than the people around you.

## THE VERY UNSAINTLY "SAINTS" IN THE NEW TESTAMENT

A lot of New Testament tension resolves itself when we keep in mind this Old Testament aspect of holiness. For instance, Paul calls all the believers in Corinth "saints" (1 Corinthians 1:2; 6:1-2) even though they were becoming notorious for factionalism, incest, lawsuits, idolatry, and prostitution.[5] Such behavior among saints was inconsistent with their calling, and Paul was writing to straighten them out. The Corinthian Christians hadn't ceased to be saints because they were acting like sinners, however. They were unworthy saints, but there had never—nor has there since—been a worthy one. That's the whole point of the gospel, grounded in the ideas of the Old Testament. The "saints" of the New Testament are very much like the tent pegs of the Tabernacle. There's nothing very remarkable about us except that we were chosen to be close to God, integrally a part of worship in his presence.

Peter makes this point by drawing attention to several Old Testament passages as he explains the relationship Christians have to God and one another. Piling together descriptions of Israel found in Exodus, Deuteronomy, Isaiah, and Hosea (represented here in small caps), Peter says,

But you are A CHOSEN RACE, a royal PRIESTHOOD, A HOLY NATION, A PEOPLE FOR God's OWN POSSESSION, so that you may proclaim the excellencies of Him who has called you out of darkness into His marvelous light; for you once were NOT A PEOPLE, but now you are THE PEOPLE OF GOD; you had NOT RECEIVED MERCY, but now you have RECEIVED MERCY.

1 PETER 2:9-10

The point is unmistakable: All who have received mercy from God in Christ now comprise the people of God, set apart for his purposes in the world. The early saints were not remarkable in themselves, but they were chosen by God.

Paul makes a similar point in Ephesians 2, when he says to the Gentile believers in his audience,

You are no longer strangers and aliens, but you are fellow citizens with the saints, and are of God's household, having been built on the foundation of the apostles and prophets, Christ Jesus Himself being the corner stone, in whom the whole building, being fitted together, is growing into *a holy temple* in the Lord, in whom you also are being built together into a dwelling of God in the Spirit.

EPHESIANS 2:19-22

According to Paul's gospel of reconciliation, Jews and Gentiles now comprise one people belonging to God and one another. He describes them as a "holy temple" because God dwells in and among them as their God (1 Corinthians

3:16-17). Again, this is not a commentary on their moral conduct but a description of their relationship with God and one another. They have been taken from common circulation in the world and set apart—*together*—for God's purposes in God's presence.

This is what Christians in the first century meant when they called each other "saints" (or described one another as "holy"). This is not to say that being a saint had nothing to do with moral excellence. There was certainly conduct befitting a saint (see especially Ephesians 5:3 and 1 Peter 2:9-12). Excellent moral conduct did not make a person saintly, however. God made people saints by saving them through his Son, Jesus. Jews and Gentiles became one people—the people of God—at the Cross according to God's gracious purposes in Christ. Good conduct followed salvation as the saints learned what it meant to live as God's holy people.

## WHAT DOES IT MEAN TO BE A SAINT TODAY?

I have conducted a rigorously *un*scientific poll to probe what modern Christians think about when they hear the word *saints*. Basically, I asked a handful of my friends who work in vocational ministry what came into their minds when I said the word. These are astute people who know the gospel and spend lots of time teaching it to others. For all of them, the word *saint* carries a note of moral exceptionalism. Saints are not just virtuous (that's the *moral* part); they are more virtuous than the rest of us (that's the *exceptional* part).

I've also found an interesting tension. These same friends also know ("in their heads," you might say) that the word *saints* was also used in the New Testament to describe *all Christians*. They know, for instance, that Paul called the Corinthians "saints," though the Christians in Corinth were anything but exceptional. In other words, they hold a contradictory belief that *saints* describes *all of us in Christ* while simultaneously describing *only a few of us in Christ*. It's a contradiction in their thinking, but in their defense, they didn't have an opportunity to read this chapter before answering my question.

I think that many people today walk through life with the same conflicting beliefs about being a saint. We know-*ish* that the word was used to describe *all* Christians in the New Testament, but we also deeply believe a person should only be called a saint if they are really, really good. We would never call ourselves saints, and we usually never call anyone else one. When we do, it's an intentional exaggeration. ("Thanks for loaning me twenty dollars. You're a saint!")

Our reluctance to use this word is significant: It means we have muted our proclamation of the gospel. In the early church, it was a clear and concise way to say, "God has saved us all and brought us together." Calling the Christians around you "saints"—or even "God's people"—can be a punchy proclamation of the gospel.[6]

## THE SAINTS ARE THOSE WHO SURROUND YOU

As I was working on this chapter, my wife, Kristy, and I experienced one of the most devasting losses a parent can face. We walked into our living room to find our fifteen-year-old daughter, Lauren, unresponsive in her stroller. Lauren lived with cerebral palsy from a birth injury, so she was no stranger to sudden, often serious, medical emergencies. This one was different, however. She wasn't simply unresponsive; she wasn't breathing. The emergency personnel who arrived at our home could not revive Lauren right away, so they rushed her to the emergency room at our local hospital. Only after she was admitted were the doctors able to raise her pulse again. She had been without oxygen for more than thirty-five minutes.

Kristy and I spent the next two days reconciling ourselves to a reality that had been all but certain from the beginning. Lauren had experienced brain death, a total cessation of all brain function because of oxygen deprivation. She was pronounced dead after only two days in the hospital.

In light of all that I have said in this chapter, I would like you to consider this question: What role do the saints play in a situation as desperate as this? Some people might think that you should pray to a (canonized, venerated) saint in a situation like this. Others might take consolation in the thought that Lauren is now in heaven with the (departed, glorified) saints around God's throne. I would like to offer an alternative view: The saints are the people of God who surround us in the moments and months of our deepest anguish.

Scores of saints entered our front door in the days after Lauren died. They provided us with tangible support in the form of meals, gift cards, flowers, and offers to help in any way possible. This is precisely what the saints of the New Testament did for one another. In fact, if you read every instance in the New Testament where the word *saints* was used to identify the people of God, you would assume that the word basically means "the people who surround you when times get difficult." Consider these examples from the New Testament:

> At present, however, I am going to Jerusalem *bringing aid to the saints*. For Macedonia and Achaia have been pleased to make some *contribution for the poor among the saints* at Jerusalem.
>
> ROMANS 15:25-26, ESV

> Concerning *the collection for the saints*, as I directed the churches of Galatia, so do you also. On the first day of every week each one of you is to put aside and save, as he may prosper, so that no collections be made when I come.
>
> I CORINTHIANS 16:1-2

> We make known to you, brothers and sisters, the grace of God given to the churches of Macedonia, that during a severe ordeal of suffering, their abundant joy and their extreme poverty have

overflowed in the wealth of their generosity. For
I testify, they gave according to their means and
beyond their means. They did so voluntarily,
begging us with great earnestness for the blessing
and fellowship of *helping the saints*.

2 CORINTHIANS 8:1-4, NET

As these passages indicate, the saints are the people of
God who surround you and support you in your distress.

Bill is one of the saints who surrounded us when Lauren
died. He's a custodian at our church who had just begun a
much-deserved two-week vacation when he heard the news
of Lauren's passing. He broke off his vacation to set up and
supervise the church building for Lauren's memorial service
because he loves us.

Karla and Grace took care of the details of Lauren's memorial at the church. They worked through the weekend to do
so, even though the church does not typically hold funeral
services on weekends. In our case, the following week was
a national holiday, so the church staff rallied around us to
make it happen.

Our pastor, Todd, returned the honorarium we gave him
for officiating the service. He said, "Thank you for the note,
but this is unnecessary." He is one of the saints who surrounded us.

Our other pastor, Bruce, agreed to offer the closing prayer
and benediction at the service because of his love for Lauren
and her love for him. Bruce had just been diagnosed with

stage 4 tongue cancer and was scheduled to begin radiation two days later.

Kim, Barb, and Jim set up and served a meal for our entire extended family after the graveside ceremony. They brought enough food to feed your extended family too.

Rachael set up a meal train for us, and twenty-eight people jumped on board to provide for our ongoing needs. The people on that meal train are a lot like the people you find on an Amtrak train: ordinary. Saints are ordinary people who surround you when the world grows dark.

I could go on like this for another page or two, but I would inevitably leave out so many who sacrificed their time, effort, and money to surround us with loving support in the days after we lost Lauren. I hope the point is sufficiently made, however: Saints don't stand apart from you because of their exceptional behavior. They stand with you in your time of greatest need. The saints are not the ones who precede you in death but the ones who help you walk through the valley of the shadow of death. They recognize you as one of their people—*one of God's people*—so they stand with you in your trouble.

When the earliest Christians talked about one another as "saints," this is what they had in mind. Many of them had been cut off from their own families because of their faith, but they found themselves surrounded by other believers who said, "You are one of us. We are God's people." They did not stand out from one another. They stood by one another. The same is (or could be) true of us today. You are among the saints. You are surrounded by the people of God. We have resources of hope and help that have come to us from Christ, and we belong to one another as the people of God. When the world goes dark, the saints surround you.

# DISCIPLES

*What We Called the Other People*
*Who Had Surrendered to Christ as Lord*

For most of my adult life, I have worked with The Navigators, a missional organization that is focused on interpersonal evangelism and discipleship. The organization's motto is "To know Christ, make Him known, and help others do the same." This commitment to helping others know Christ and make him known grew out of founder Dawson Trotman's observation that many people in the early twentieth century were winning souls for Christ but few were helping new believers grow in maturity.

Trotman observed that one key attribute of maturity in any living thing was its ability to reproduce. If new believers were born again at their initial conversion but failed to grow in godliness to the point that they could help another person come to Christ and grow in faith, something was amiss. We are, after all, "born to reproduce," as Trotman put it in one of his most enduring messages. Where there was no growth toward maturity, there was no way to fulfill the great commission. Only a disciple could heed Jesus' command to "make disciples of all the nations" (Matthew 28:19). It takes one to make one, as the saying goes. So by accident, design, trial, and error, The Navigators pioneered disciplemaking practices in the United States and helped put this idea on the map for the church.

Dawson Trotman didn't invent the concept of discipleship or disciplemaking methods. But he did help mainstream the idea within the church to the point that you would have to look hard to find a church or Christian organization today that doesn't put discipleship somewhere near the center of its vision or mission statement. From discipleship programs to discipleship pastors, everyone seems committed to discipleship in our day.

Or are we?

Somehow, despite our express commitment to discipleship, most Christians would be hard-pressed to define what the word means. We seem to have put the great commission and the idea of discipleship firmly in place without a clear sense of what it *means* to be a disciple. If this point seems doubtful, scratch out your own mental definition and keep reading. As you do so, consider this: The word *discipleship* isn't even found in the Bible. The earliest Christians called one another "disciples," but they never talked about "discipleship." Christians today talk almost exclusively about "discipleship" and almost never refer to one another as "disciples." The words of the imminent theologian, Inigo Montoya, the drunken Spanish swordsman from *The Princess Bride*, come to mind: "You keep using that word. I do not think it means what you think it means."[1]

## A SKETCH OF "DISCIPLES" IN THE GOSPELS

Anyone familiar with the New Testament would likely turn to the Gospels to discover what they can about being a "disciple." After all, the term is used over 230 times in the Gospels, and 73 times in the Gospel of Matthew alone. Sometimes Matthew has the apostles in view (Matthew 10:1; 20:17; 26:35; and 28:16), but often enough, he presents his readers with a wider company of people who followed Jesus around. In fact, it seems like one of the primary occupations of all disciples, whether the apostles or the larger group, involved walking around with Jesus from place to place, listening to him teach, and high-fiving one another when he owned the Pharisees. A casual reader could be forgiven for assuming that being a "disciple" meant "walking around with Jesus."

In fact, the willingness to drop everything and do whatever Jesus asked seemed to be the dividing line that set the disciples apart from the crowd of curious onlookers who were drawn to Jesus. Notice that each of these statements from

Jesus is made after some reference is made to the "crowds" who were following him:

> When Jesus saw a crowd around Him, He gave orders to depart to the other side of the sea. Then a scribe came and said to Him, "Teacher, I will follow You wherever You go." Jesus said to him, "The foxes have holes and the birds of the air have nests, but the Son of Man has nowhere to lay His head." Another of the disciples said to Him, "Lord, permit me first to go and bury my father." But Jesus said to him, "Follow Me, and allow the dead to bury their own dead."
>
> When He got into the boat, His disciples followed Him.
>
> MATTHEW 8:18-23

> Large crowds were going along with Him; and He turned and said to them, "If anyone comes to Me, and does not hate his own father and mother and wife and children and brothers and sisters, yes, and even his own life, he cannot be My disciple. Whoever does not carry his own cross and come after Me cannot be My disciple.
>
> LUKE 14:25-27

It's difficult to open any page of any Gospel and try to find a scene where Jesus is not with his disciples. Matthew briefly describes one such scene where Jesus "made the disciples get into the boat and go ahead of Him to the other side [of the Sea of Galilee], while He sent the crowds away. After He had sent the crowds away, He went up on the mountain by Himself to pray; and when it was evening, He was there alone" (Matthew 14:22-23). The passage draws attention to itself because Jesus was seldom portrayed alone (though Luke 5:16 makes it clear that he often withdrew to pray).

From the Sermon on the Mount to the garden of Gethsemane, his ministry is portrayed as itinerant work with his disciples, often among crowds of people. The disciples seemingly shared in everything he did. Apart from brief periods of extended, solitary prayer, it seems that Jesus never left them, and they never left him until the night of his arrest. The Gospel writers do not emphasize any extended times of separation. The only coming and going involved coming to Jesus and going wherever he went. No sketch of a "disciple" in the Gospels can proceed without acknowledging this basic point.

The Gospel writers do add a twist to this simple sketch, though, and it takes us to another essential characteristic of a "disciple" in the Gospels. Disciples didn't merely congregate around Jesus. Crowds did that, but crowds came and went, especially when Jesus' teaching got hard. The disciples, on the other hand, staked everything on Jesus' word. He could ask them to do difficult or incongruous things, and they were expected to do them just because he said so. Disciples didn't drift away because of growing disillusionment with

Jesus. Fickleness characterized the crowds. Disciples stuck with Jesus no matter what he taught or asked of them. Once, when disgruntled crowds were bailing on him, Jesus asked the disciples if they wanted to leave too. Peter answered for all, saying, "Lord, to whom shall we go? You have words of eternal life. We have believed and have come to know that You are the Holy One of God" (John 6:68-69).

For a few, like Nicodemus and Joseph of Arimathea, surrender took time. For others, surrender marked the start of their relationship with Jesus. For all of them, it was conclusive. An earnest supplicant like the rich young ruler might walk away from Jesus (Mark 10:17-31), but a disciple never would. A halfhearted disciple might walk away (John 6:66), but a true disciple never would (John 8:31).

It is fair to say that the call to be a disciple was itself a call to surrender. As Jesus put it, "If anyone wishes to come after Me, he must deny himself, and take up his cross daily and follow Me. For whoever wishes to save his life will lose it, but whoever loses his life for My sake, he is the one who will save it" (Luke 9:23-24). Though the Greek word for "disciple," *mathētēs*, is related to the Greek verb meaning "to learn" (*manthanō*), it would be a mistake of the first order to say that two words mean the same thing because they share the same root.[2] A cursory reading of the Gospels will show you that disciples were not summoned to *come and learn* but to *come and die*.

This should make us wary of any suggestion that discipleship is a process or a program of study leading to maturity.

That's often what we mean today by *discipleship*, but this concept does not appear to arise from the New Testament. If the early church had been introduced to the word *discipleship*, I think they would have assumed it was a relational term, like *brotherhood*, since "disciples" were manifestly people in relationship with Jesus. This may be one of the most important takeaways for a Christian today: *Discipleship* is a relational term, and it implies surrender to Jesus.

## WHEN JESUS WENT TO HEAVEN, THERE WERE STILL DISCIPLES ON EARTH

In the book of Acts, *disciple* was a common form of self-designation among Christians. In fact, Luke is the one who tells us that "*the disciples* were first called Christians in Antioch" (Acts 11:26). Before anyone else called us "Christians," we apparently called ourselves "disciples." By the numbers, Luke used the word *disciples* (Greek *mathētēs*) twenty-eight times and the word *Christians* (Greek *christianos*) only twice in Acts. The word *Christians*, as I mentioned in the introduction to this book, was a term outsiders used about the church. Even after this term was coined, the Christians seem to have ignored it and kept calling each other "disciples." (And, interestingly, though "disciples" is used over 250 times in the Gospels and Acts, it isn't used in any of the New Testament letters.)

That means that Christians in the earliest days of the church saw continuity between the experience, relationship, and commitments the original disciples had with Jesus and those who believed in him because of their testimony.[3] They recognized surrender and adherence to Jesus as Lord when they saw it. This is what made a person a "disciple" and bound them together as a community of disciples in their day. The same thing is true two thousand years later.

Imagine what changes might come about in your church or small group if you stopped calling one another Christians for a year and only referred to one another as "disciples." If you decide to try this out, please read this entire chapter first. It might be an appropriate experiment to run, but only if people have in mind what Luke had in mind when he used the word *disciple* in the book of Acts.

## YOU HAVE NEVER MET A CHRISTIAN WHO IS NOT A DISCIPLE

If you think about the way your church's staff or programs are structured, you might think of evangelism and discipleship as two different things. The pastor or program for evangelism is there to help people become Christians. The pastor or program for discipleship is there to help Christians become, well, disciples. The only problem with this structure is that it's misleading. The very first reference to "Christians" in the Bible, Acts 11:26 (quoted above), should make us wary of drawing any significant distinction between "Christians" (or "converts") and "disciples." You have never met a convert who is not a disciple. The assumption that a person can believe in Jesus as Savior and Lord without being a disciple is a mistake. You cannot open to any page of Scripture and construct an argument that a person can become a Christian without being a disciple. Well-known scholar and pastor John Piper has said it this way:

> The word *disciple* in the New Testament does not mean a second-stage Christian . . . as if there were converts, then there are disciples who are little stage-two Christians who learn more, and then there are disciple makers.
>
> Now all those groupings are linguistically foreign to the New Testament. A disciple in the New Testament is simply a Christian. . . . Everybody that was converted to Jesus was a disciple. Everybody that was converted to Jesus was a Christian.[4]

You become a disciple because of the grace of God through faith in Christ. You become a disciple in the same way you become a "brother" or "sister," by being born again into the family of God. You do not become a disciple by going through a course on discipleship any more than you become a brother by taking a course on brotherhood. A course might help you become a better brother, and a plan for growth might help you become a better disciple. No plan, program, or practice can make you a disciple, though. Only Christ can do that.

What is more, in the same way that you can be an immature brother or sister without ceasing to be a sibling, you can be an immature disciple without ceasing to be a disciple. Discipleship is not synonymous with maturity, though all disciples will grow in the grace of God. They won't be able to help becoming more like Jesus as they say yes to everything he asks and because he is with them continually. Jesus is their Lord. The authority of Jesus' word and mission will become increasingly evident in their lives. They are not called "disciples" because of their maturity or mission, however. They are disciples because of their relationship with their Master.

## BEING A DISCIPLE TODAY

Whenever we suggest that disciples are the more mature, above-average Christians, we imply that people can become converts to Christianity without surrendering their lives to Christ as Lord. No one in the first-century church would have understood using that word in that way. The wholehearted surrender of unworthy people to the merciful Son of God, who is Lord of all, constituted what we now call "discipleship." They called one another "disciples" not because they had grown but because they had died. Let me explain.

When I was a graduate teaching assistant at Auburn University a few decades ago, I had the privilege of working with a very sharp student assistant from Japan named Shohei. He had become curious about Christianity and had heard Christians say that non-Christians were spiritually "dead" (Ephesians 2:1). Over coffee one day, this student asked me point-blank: "When you look at me, do you think, *That guy, Shohei, he is a dead person!*"?

I was taken aback by Shohei's directness, and I can't remember whether I gave him an answer that was as clear and direct as his question. I'm pretty sure I told him, "Yes, in a manner of speaking, those who do not know Christ are dead."

Here is what I have learned since then: Those who *do* know Christ are also dead, in a manner of speaking. If we have come to know Jesus as Lord, we have died to ourselves. There is, in fact, no other way to relate to Jesus as Lord than to die to yourself. As Paul says, "I have been crucified with Christ; and it is no longer I who live, but Christ lives in me; and the life which I now live in the flesh I live by faith in the Son of God, who loved me and gave Himself up for me" (Galatians 2:20). Jesus himself made it clear that no one could follow him as a disciple (i.e., a Christian) who was not willing to "take up his cross daily" (Luke 9:23).

Whenever you find yourself in a community of disciples, you are in a community of common surrender. Disciples—Christians—are those who have said no to the life they sought to attain to say yes to the life Jesus offers. They have willingly laid their lives down because Jesus Christ is Lord. Calling one another "disciples" today reminds us of this reality.

Earlier in this chapter, I alluded to an idea that I want to circle back to. What effect would it have on your church or small group if you started calling each other "disciples," exclusively, instead of "Christians"? You could try this out for a month or a year, if you'd like, but I am only asking you to run this as a thought experiment for the moment. How would your believing friends react if you started calling them "disciples"?

I imagine that many would feel intimidated. They might even voice an objection in the same way they would if you called them "saints." Many of us have internalized the idea that a "disciple" is a next-level Christian. If you started calling your friends "disciples," they might feel like you didn't really know them. Or worse, that you were putting them under pressure to prove themselves (which would be ironic, given everything we've observed about Jesus' disciples and the meaning of the word). Disciples of Jesus bring nothing but surrender into their relationship with the Lord.

If people squirm when you use the term, remind them that *disciple* doesn't mean "super Christian." You can tell them that *disciple* is one of the miracle terms of the Bible. We did not make ourselves disciples; God did! Disciples are with Jesus because of his grace, not their résumés. Disciples are marked by surrender, not success. They have decided that death with Jesus is preferable to life without him. They are the ones who say yes to Jesus and don't walk away when his teaching gets hard.

When my first wife passed away, I struggled through a very deep valley of grief. All the dreams I had for my future had involved being with her. I lost my orientation to the future when I lost her, and I was bone-tired most of the time. I discovered immediately that I had no stamina for the kind of campus ministry I had done for fifteen years. I could drive to campus, talk with one student, and be wiped out for the rest of the day.

Amid this struggle, I began doing some financial calculations. It dawned on me that I might be able to retire early if I played my cards right. I was still in my forties, so I would have to figure out a way to make it fifteen more years in some ministry capacity or with some other source of income. Even so, early retirement seemed like it might be an option. I spent weeks doing the math. (I am an English major, after all.) Then I spent months leaning into this dream of early retirement. But the Lord woke me up.

I believe I was driving to campus, talking to myself about "fifteen more years of ministry, then early retirement" when the Lord spoke to me. His words were something like this: "Thank you for offering to give me fifteen more years of your life. Could I have all of them instead?" As only a word from God can do, he broke my heart and lifted my burden in a moment. He rebuked my self-love and invited me into fellowship with a word. This is the experience of discipleship, the call to come and die.

Only a few months later, I shared this illustration from my life at a student conference in New Zealand. The memory was still so fresh, I could hardly speak without tears. (Kiwis are not known for strong emotion, so I was trying to keep it together.) When I finished speaking, a young woman came up to me and said, "That message was for me. I don't know what the Lord is asking of me right now, but I know I have been focusing on the security and wealth a new job could bring me. Thank you for sharing your story. I needed that."

This is what it looks like to share your life within a gospel-shaped community: One believer helping another say no to self and yes to Jesus. This is the fellowship of common surrender. This is discipleship.

# FELLOW WORKERS

*The Words We Made Up
to Show We Were in This Together*

As I write this chapter, I have just finished watching *The Bear*, an award-winning TV series about a master chef who returns home to Chicago to run his deceased brother's restaurant. The place is a picture of barely tolerable workplace dysfunction. The restaurant is filthy, the finances are in shambles, and relationships between the old workers and new management are nearly un*bear*able. (See what I did there?) In fact, the language in the show was so abusive, I only made it halfway through the fourth episode of season 1 before I tapped out. (This is what I mean when I say I "finished watching *The Bear*.")

Even so, you only have to stay engaged with the show for a few minutes to witness a scene that could hold its own as a spiritual parable. In it, Carmen (played by Jeremy Allen White), the new owner of The Original Beef of Chicagoland, keeps referring to everyone in the kitchen as "Chef." Some are confused. Others are belligerent, and no one is more annoyed than his pugilistic cousin, Richie (played by Ebon Moss-Bachrach). After Carmen tells all the "chefs" to clean their stations, Richie yells, "Does anyone know what he's saying?"

Without skipping a beat Carmen replies, "I refer to everybody as Chef because it's a sign of respect." It doesn't take long—at least no longer than halfway through episode 4—before everyone is calling everyone else "Chef" at The Original Beef of Chicagoland. Their relationships are not all cordial, to be sure, but there's a positive trajectory that mirrors this change in direct address. *The Bear* acts out a drama we all experience in real life: The words we use shape the world we live in. If this is true on the plane of everyday human experience, how much more so within the church!

We see this dynamic working in the early church, as people began referring to one another as *co*workers, *co*heirs, *co*prisoners, and the like. The writers of the New Testament put the Greek prefix *syn-*, here translated as "co-" or "fellow," to work modifying all kinds of nouns. They believed God had bound Christians together into a community of common purpose at the Cross. They proclaimed the gospel of reconciliation with a prefix.

## FELLOW (FILL-IN-THE-BLANK)-ERS

The English prefix *co-* works in much the same way its Greek counterpart *syn-* does. You can prefix *co-* to any number of nouns in English to shift the meaning:

- pilot becomes copilot
- patriot becomes compatriot
- laborer becomes collaborator
- conspirator becomes coconspirator

I love that last example. It is fabulous for its redundancy. Both *co* and *con* mean "together with." We find similar examples in the New Testament, as we will see. The important thing to observe is that the prefix *co-* in English, like the prefix *syn-* in Greek, signifies that people are in it together, whatever "it" happens to be.[1] Outside the Gospels and Acts, the New Testament writers use this prefix over thirty times to refer to specific Christians, groups, or all believers. When our faith was young, here is a sample of what we called each other in Scripture:

- fellow workers (fourteen times)
- fellow prisoners (three times)
- fellow partakers (three times)
- fellow servants/slaves (three times)
- fellow soldiers (twice)
- fellow citizens (once)

- fellow members (once)
- fellow sharers (once)
- fellow elect (once)[2]

From this representative list, it seems that you could be a "fellow just-about-anything" to other believers in the early church. Whatever circumstance you found yourself in as a Christian, you were bound together with other believers. In fact, the list above could be extended somewhat.

If you were traveling together with an offering for another community, you were "fellow travelers" with the Christians accompanying you (see similar language in 2 Corinthians 8:19). I'm not sure there was any spiritual connotation to this word, but I wish there were. If you were serving as a church leader alongside other church leaders, you were a "fellow elder" (1 Peter 5:1). The angel who appeared to John in the book of Revelation identified himself twice as John's "fellow servant" (Revelation 19:10; 22:9) who should not be worshiped, even though he was resplendent. There is so much variety in the group of "fellow _____" terms in the New Testament, it is hard to know which ones to include in the list.

What is clear, however, is that the Greek prefix *syn-* places an energetic emphasis on the togetherness Christians shared because of the Cross of Christ. When Paul explained the mystery of the gospel to the Ephesians, he said that "Gentiles are *fellow heirs* and *fellow members* of the body, and *fellow partakers* of the promise in Christ Jesus through the gospel" (Ephesians 3:6). In the Greek, that sentence reads like a three-prefix pileup. Coupled with Paul's earlier insistence that Gentiles are "fellow citizens with the saints" (Ephesians 2:19), the point is impossible to miss. The gospel had brought people together into an unlikely but unmistakable community, not because of their goodwill but because of the grace of God. Through the Cross of Christ, formerly separated people are now in it together, whether "it" involved suffering, missionary work, or service within a community.

The words that join forces in Paul's *syn-* constructions in Ephesians are fascinating. Take Paul's insistence that Jews and Gentiles are both "fellow members of the body." Have you ever looked at your right foot and thought of it as a "fellow member of your body, together with your left foot"? The word *member* already carries the connotation that something is part of a larger whole. You don't add *meaning* to the word *member* by calling someone a "fellow member"—you add *emphasis*.

The same could be said of "fellow citizens." All citizens are "fellow citizens" by virtue of belonging to the same state. This also holds true for "fellow heirs." If a person passes away with no spouse, multiple children, and no will, inheritance laws divide the estate between the *heirs*. No law code calls them "fellow heirs" or "coheirs" because doing so would be redundant. That's what I love about this set of terms for self-designation in the New Testament. The sheer redundancy of calling believers "fellow members," "fellow citizens," "fellow heirs," and "fellow sharers" emphatically proclaims the reconciling power of the gospel. This is the gospel in a prefix![3]

If you look back at the list, you will notice that the first term, *fellow workers*, stands out because of the number of times it appears. If there was one thing the early church members believed they had in common with one another, it was the work that Jesus had entrusted to them. In the New Testament letters, a person was about twice as likely to be called a "fellow worker" as a "fellow (anything-else)-er." It's worth raising a question about this prominent term of self-designation as we proceed though: Did all believers consider all *other* believers to be coworkers in the same way they considered one another to be brothers and sisters, saints, et cetera? For some scholars, this is an open-and-shut case. For me, it's an open question.

## FELLOW WORKERS

The "fellow worker" passages of the New Testament tend to cluster at the close of Paul's letters, the places where it feels most like we are reading someone else's personal mail. We tend to skim these portions of the letters and think very little about statements like these:

> Greet Prisca and Aquila, my fellow workers in Christ Jesus.
> ROMANS 16:3

> Epaphras, my fellow prisoner in Christ Jesus, greets you, as do Mark, Aristarchus, Demas, Luke, my fellow workers.
> PHILEMON 1:23-24

A person surveying Paul's letters could be forgiven for assuming Paul only uses the term *fellow workers* to refer to other vocational missionaries like himself because Paul clearly does this sort of thing. In fact, Joseph Hellerman says, "Συνεργός [*Synergos*; "fellow worker"], unlike ἀδελφός [*adelphos*; "brother" or "sister"], is *not used of believers in general* . . . [but] primarily of associates on [Paul's] mission team."[4] Dr. Hellerman wrote the book on the use of "brothers and sisters" in the New Testament, and I am inclined to respect his judgment. There are a few passages that make a definitive statement like this less plausible, however.

In his letter to Philemon, for instance, Paul calls Philemon a "fellow worker" (Philemon 1:1) even though Philemon was not a traveling missionary with Paul at this point. Some people think Paul refers to him this way because Philemon had been on one of Paul's mission teams. That is plausible but not proven. It could simply be that everyone who believed in Jesus as Lord shared in the work of Jesus and could be identified as a "fellow worker." A person might be mobile or local. The deciding factor might simply be whether they believed in Jesus as Lord and, thus, took part in his work.

The same kind of question can be raised in Philippians, where Paul addresses three or four leaders in the congregation along with "the rest of my fellow workers, whose names are in the book of life" (Philippians 4:3). Paul could be referring to a subset of Philippian believers who once worked with him as missionaries. Arguing this way basically assumes that "fellow workers" can't be a general reference to all believers though.

If we assume the opposite, the verse makes better sense: Paul is simply greeting the whole church as "fellow workers" whose names are all found in the Book of Life. This isn't too great a stretch if we recall that Paul says he is a fellow worker *with the Corinthians* for their joy (2 Corinthians 1:24). In his commentary on this passage, New Testament lecturer Colin Kruse says this is "a most attractive description of the purpose of Christian ministry: to work alongside people to increase their joy!"[5] I am inclined to think that "fellow worker" is not a technical reference to people who traveled on Paul's missionary teams but a general reference to all believers. We call them "fellow workers" because we work alongside them all or, perhaps, because every believer is a *potential* fellow worker. When you come into their orbit of life, you become *actual* fellow workers.

As a final example, consider how John uses the term *fellow workers* in his third letter. John urges a local Christian community to show hospitality to traveling missionaries with these words: "Therefore we ought to support such men, so that we may be fellow workers with the truth" (3 John 1:8). That is, the Christians living in this town showed themselves to be "fellow workers" by feeding and housing those who were traveling around preaching the gospel. It wasn't the itinerant missionaries but the local believers whom John identified as "fellow workers." The potential for partnership in the gospel makes us all "fellow workers."

I don't mean to overplay my hand here. Paul certainly referred to people on his mission teams (past or present) as his "fellow workers." This would have been quite natural because they all worked closely together. Their potential for partnership *had been* realized. But I think there is good sense in referring to all believers as "fellow workers" because God has already established the basis for collaboration within his Kingdom. If I have occasion to address you (or vice versa), you have come into the orbit of my experience. We are in this work together.

## WHO ARE YOUR COWORKERS?

One of the largest boots in the world—a size 638 ½ D (US)—can be found in the small town of Red Wing, Minnesota. That's because Red Wing Shoe Company has been headquartered there since 1905. What better way to commemorate your global success in making footwear than to construct a twenty-foot-tall leather boot?[6] One day, I walked past the giant boot in Red Wing's flagship retail store, and I decided to peruse the small museum of the company's shoemaking history. As I looked at photographs of the various company workers, I wondered whether tanners who deal with raw leather in a factory in the United States think of themselves as coworkers with the Dutch folks who serve at the corporate office in Amsterdam. Or whether the sales floor staff in Riyadh, Saudi Arabia, think of themselves as working with their counterparts in Tokyo. Chances are pretty good *they don't*, and chances are also pretty good *the owners* of the company *do*. Whether each employee knows it or not, they are all working under the supervision of company owners who are purposefully coordinating efforts to reach a common goal. If that's not what it means to be a coworker, I'm not sure what is.

From the perspective of "upper management" in the church, we are all working alongside one another for the attainment of a common goal. Though we may be spread throughout the world and occupied with a great variety of tasks, we are "fellow workers" just as definitely as we are "fellow citizens" and "fellow members" of the body. This is not the result of our decision but of God's. Better yet, it's the result of God's grace poured out on us at the Cross of Christ. We are surrounded by "fellows" in the same way we are surrounded by "saints." Whether we have been commissioned to cross a continent or a cubicle, whether we are translating a Bible into another language or reading it to our grandkids, what matters is that we recognize ourselves as workers and realize we are not alone.

God has graciously brought you into a great company of fellow workers. Do you see them? Your careful planning did not bring these partnerships about, but your careful planning and deliberate action are most certainly called for now. This is precisely the kind of thing you would expect from God: He has a penchant for collaborating with his creatures (as we saw in chapter 1). From the Garden of Eden to the present day, he works by opening to us opportunities that were previously impossible or even unthinkable. No wonder he has reconfigured our relationships so that we can work together. Every believer you encounter has the potential to help you accomplish the "good works, which God prepared beforehand so that [you] would walk in them" (Ephesians 2:10). If you're not working, that's a problem. If you're working alone, that may be a problem too. If all your partnerships are predictable, developed along lines of natural affinity that make sense to everyone in the world, something is probably amiss. You are part of the church, not a social club.

Who is walking with you? Who is working alongside you? What keeps you from active, intentional fellowship with your fellow workers, fellow citizens, and "fellow sharers in the tribulation and kingdom and steadfastness in Jesus" (Revelation 1:9, author's translation)?

For me, it is the gravitational pull toward isolation and independent work. I like to be left alone. I try to sneak hours of solitude into my workdays. Sometimes I don't answer the phone when my own mother calls. What about you? Does the idea of joining with Jesus and others in the work sound tiring? Does it feel like one more task to add to an already endless list of things to do? Does it seem unattractive because all your other pursuits seem more fun or pressing? Does it make you feel anxious? Or small? Or condemned?

Here is what you must know: You aren't designed to deal with these feelings alone. You need Jesus, of course, but you also need your "fellow sharers" in the grace of God. You were not designed to stand alone or cycle through life with people who are lost. You cannot find your way through this world by yourself. You belong with a community of people who have in common surrender to Jesus. You need such a community to work, worship, and suffer with, and thankfully, you don't have to create it. If you know Jesus Christ as Lord, grace has already found you, and God will provide you with fellowship. You need to be careful not to look for it only among the people who are like you (and who like you). Your community is comprised not of Democrats or Republicans, rich or poor, blue collar or white collar but of saints, beloved fellow workers, disciples, brothers and sisters. You can even call them "Christians" if you want to.

# 10

# CHRISTIANS

*What Others Called Us*
*When We Were Despised and Dispossessed*

God created the world with his word. Then he redeemed the world with his Word, Jesus Christ. He's so good at this that I am convinced he can redeem the word *Christian*. When people first started using it, it certainly needed redemption. When our faith was young, calling someone a "Christian" wasn't a compliment. It was not a label but a libel, on the lips of people who did not like the Christian faith.[1] As we have noted before, it was probably coined by people in the city of Syrian Antioch (see Acts 11:26). The word took a jab at the crazies who had staked their life and eternity on a certain "Christ." Of course, that meant the word was one part description and one part derision, a less-than-gracious label you could throw at someone involved in a sect you didn't understand.

Calling believers by an unflattering name has happened regularly throughout history. The followers of Martin Luther were called Luther-*ans*, not as a compliment. The followers of Menno Simons became known as Menno-*nites*. Not a compliment. The followers of John Calvin became known as Calvin-*ists*. Also not a compliment. You see the pattern.

It may be hard for modern Christians to wrap their minds around this, but the word *Christian* was initially a slur, a slight, an accusation. When you read the word *Christian* in the only three passages in the New Testament where it is mentioned—Acts 11:26; Acts 26:28; and 1 Peter 4:15-16—remember that Christians were being *distinguished* in a very *undistinguished* way with the term. So when did Christians choose to adopt this negative term as a form of self-designation?

While we cannot pinpoint a day or a year, the second or third generation of believers were clearly wearing this term of derision as a badge of honor. They began using *Christian* to describe *themselves* within the church. In effect, they said to their detractors, "You wanted to weaken us with an insulting label. We accept! The name you gave us connects us to the name of our Lord." They had never been ashamed to be associated with Christ.

## THE USE OF "CHRISTIAN" BEYOND THE NEW TESTAMENT

You cannot survey the New Testament to discover when, where, and why Christians began to designate themselves "Christians." Instead, you must look at Christian writings just after the close of the New Testament era. We call the earliest collection of them *The Apostolic Fathers*. These compositions are not sacred Scripture in any Christian tradition, though some of them were very highly regarded in their day. Many of the authors were (or were thought to be) contemporaries of the apostles themselves. Their writings were not received in the early churches as authoritative for settling matters of doctrine, but they were respected nevertheless. I suppose people listened to the letters of the Apostolic Fathers the way you and I might listen to a gifted pastor or author today. I will quote from their writings in the paragraphs below, not because they have the authority of the apostles but because they are our spiritual forebears. We wouldn't call ourselves "Christians" today if they had not adopted the label in their generation. In this respect, we need their writings in order to understand who we are.

The term *Christian* appears in the writings of the Apostolic Fathers twenty-four times. (The word *Christianity*, which never appears in the Bible, appears in their writings another six times.) If you scan letters of the Apostolic Fathers, you get the sense that people were still being called "Christian" as an insult or accusation well into the second century. Even so, this next generation of believers adopted the insult because it associated them with Christ. If enemies insisted on hanging the name of Christ around their neck, even as a formal accusation, they were more than willing to suffer for it. That's how we should read the following statement from Ignatius of Antioch to the Roman church. He wrote this on a forced march from Syria to Rome to be executed, and he asked the believers in Rome:

> Only pray for me for strength, both inward and outward, that I may not merely speak, but also have the will, *that I may not only be called a Christian*, but may also be found to be one. For if I be found to be one, I can also be called one, and then be deemed faithful when I no longer am visible in the world [i.e., when I am killed].[2]

In this example, Ignatius was about to face trial and certain death in Rome. His legal sentence would have been a foregone conclusion unless, perhaps, he publicly recanted his faith before the governor. Instead, Ignatius took the accusation against him and told the believers in Rome to pray that he would be worthy of it! He embraced the name of "Christian" to show his unwavering fidelity to Jesus in the face of public opposition and certain death.

We find the same interplay between accusation and honor in the account of another early Christian martyr, Polycarp. When the Roman proconsul in Smyrna tried to persuade this old man to renounce his faith in Jesus before a hostile crowd, Polycarp replied:

> For eighty-six years I have been his servant,
> and [Jesus] has done me no wrong. How can I
> blaspheme my King who saved me? . . . If you vainly
> suppose that I will swear by the genius of Caesar,
> as you request, and pretend not to know who I am,
> listen carefully: *I am a Christian.* Now if you want
> to learn the doctrine of Christianity, name a day and
> give me a hearing.[3]

When Polycarp said, "Listen carefully: I am a Christian," he was not providing information to the governor. He was *accepting the accusation* that had been lodged against him. In doing so, he took on the name of Christ as a public honor he would willingly die for. The governor made sure everyone gathered in the stadium knew that Polycarp had confessed to his crimes by announcing three times: "Polycarp has confessed that he is a Christian."[4] When the people heard this, they went into a frenzy and demanded that Polycarp be burned alive, since the lions had been retired from the arena for the night.

Polycarp took a stand in the name of Christ, as a "Christian." He declared, before magistrate and masses, that he would rather suffer death than dishonor his Savior. In his day, calling yourself a "Christian" meant certain suffering and required astonishing courage. That's an attribute we would do well to reclaim.

There are still places in the world where Christians are faced with the threat of death if they do not renounce the name of Jesus. Most of us reading this book, however, live in societies where the threats are more muted and the demands are brought down a decibel. The pressure is still in there, and sometimes subtle, social pressure creates its own version of torment. No one is likely to ask you to renounce your faith; they just want you to keep quiet about it. No one will ask you to deny your religion, but they will reward your compromise.

If you want to keep calling yourself a "Christian"—and I hope you do!—try to remember the first generation of believers who took this insult and transformed it into an honor. So great was their faith in the face of death that they converted the meaning of the word *Christian*. We bear the name in our day because they were unashamed of it in theirs. May it call us back to an era of unswerving allegiance in the face of mounting pressure to back down. In fact, may it do more than call us back: May it bind us together.

## "CHRISTIANS" DIDN'T STAND ALONE

I remember reading *The Pilgrim's Progress* by John Bunyan when I was young. In this allegory, a pilgrim named Christian makes his way through a variety of dangers (like Vanity Fair and the Slough of Despond) toward the Celestial

City. Though I admire the book and its author to this day, I think it vividly presents a problem that has plagued Western Christianity. Most of us conceive of our walk with Christ as a solitary journey from earth to heaven. We imagine ourselves walking alone like Christian in *Pilgrim's Progress*. I don't think this was the way the early church thought of their journey, and I think they used to term *Christian* to signify their togetherness.

The early church was a community that stood out by standing together. In one of the earliest written defenses of the Christian faith, the (anonymous) author of "The Epistle to Diognetus" begins his letter:

> Since I see, most excellent Diognetus, that you are
> extremely interested in learning about the religion of
> the Christians and are asking very clear and careful
> questions about them—specifically, what God they
> believe in and how they worship him . . . what is the
> nature of *the heartfelt love they have for one another*;
> and why *this new race or way of life* has come into
> the world we live in now and not before—I gladly
> welcome this interest of yours.[5]

The recipient of this letter, Diognetus, seemed to be sincerely interested in "the religion of the Christians." The author of the letter knew Diognetus was principally interested in two things: the nature of Christian worship and the depth of Christian community. He refers to Christians as "this new race or way of life" as if a new people group had materialized right in front of Diognetus's eyes.

People in the Roman world knew what it was like to see groups of displaced people immigrate into their cities. Some of them had probably seen a new "race" of people forcibly repatriated from some remote, conquered land to their own neighborhoods almost overnight. No one had experienced a new race comprised of *their own family and friends* suddenly taking shape before their very eyes, however. These were not foreigners, after all, but friends. Yet, somehow, they were becoming altogether different by associating with this new mystery cult called "Christianity."

The gospel, it turns out, was reconfiguring relationships so entirely that a new family (the Greek *genos* can mean "family" as well as "race") was forming as outsiders looked on in amazement or anger. This is what the author of "The Epistle to Diognetus" emphasized later in his letter:

> *Christians* are not distinguished from the rest of
> humanity by country, language, or custom. For
> nowhere do they live in cities of their own, nor
> do they speak some unusual dialect, nor do they
> practice an eccentric way of life. . . . But while they
> live in both Greek and barbarian cities, as each one's
> lot was cast, and follow the local customs in dress
> and food and other aspects of life, at the same time
> they demonstrate *the remarkable and admittedly
> unusual character of their own citizenship.* They live

in their own countries, but only as nonresidents; they participate in everything as citizens, and endure everything as foreigners. Every foreign country is their fatherland, and every fatherland is foreign.[6]

I love this passage as much as any in the Apostolic Fathers. It captures so wonderfully what the gospel was accomplishing as a *social phenomenon* in the ancient world. It didn't make people eccentric or require them to leave home. They didn't have to move to a commune or learn a holy language to say their prayers. They didn't have to exchange their street clothes for flowing robes or chant mystical incantations when the moon was full. No, Christians stayed in their own cities, "as each one's lot was cast," but their true citizenship was changed entirely. In full view of the neighbors and siblings they had grown up around, a new race of people was born. Having never left home, they became citizens of a new Kingdom.

The thing about a kingdom is that you don't live in it by yourself. When God gave new citizenship to believers, they were immediately surrounded by new fellow citizens. The author of "The Epistle to Diognetus" knew that this made Christians stand out. In fact, he knew that the love they had for one another, where none should have expected it, was causing people to take notice.

People argued (without evidence) that Christians had weird worship practices. They were a small society that shunned the spotlight, so people assumed they had something to hide.

Christians believed there was only one God deserving of all worship, so polytheists raged against them as "atheists." (I suppose that having only one God seemed very close to having none at all.) Folks could see well enough that Christians wouldn't offer sacrifices to Caesar as a god, so they came up with stories about how they offered children as sacrifices to their god. Basically, a good bit of inconsistent, unsubstantiated propaganda was advanced to show that Christians practiced deviant and dark worship.

But no one in the ancient world could deny what they saw in broad daylight: Christians loved one another. In fact, Christians didn't just love one another; they loved the poor, the abandoned, the elderly, the sick . . . and even their enemies! One Roman emperor in the late 300s, Julian the Apostate, encouraged pagan priests to do more for strangers and the poor because their religion looked so pathetic alongside that of the "atheists" (i.e., Christians). He wrote:

> Ought we not rather to consider that the progress
> of Atheism has been principally owing to *the*
> *humanity evinced by Christians towards strangers*, to
> the reverence they have manifested towards the dead,
> and to the delusive gravity which they have assumed
> in their life? . . .
>    . . . For, while there are no persons in need among
> the Jews, and while even the impious Galileans [i.e.,
> Christians] provide *not only for those of their own party*

*who are in want, but also for those who hold with us*, it would indeed be disgraceful if we were to allow our own people to suffer from poverty.[7]

What Julian and every other person in the ancient world knew was that you could only rail against people practicing genuine compassion and supportive community for so long. People who lived with "heartfelt love . . . for one another" stood out against the dark backdrop of a cruel and self-centered world. More than that, they drew people into their orbit. No one failed to take note of this among the early Christians. In fact, this is what made Christian community stand out from all the other cults, guilds, and ethnic assemblies of the Roman world. Christians were people united to one another in true love without any bond but Christ. Christ made them Christians, not their commonality with one another. Christ brought people together and required them to love one another across the gaps of class, ethnicity, and culture. Unlike the pilgrim of John Bunyan's allegory, these people were not walking a lonely road toward the Celestial City. They were standing together in very dark times.

# THE LANGUAGE OF CHRISTIAN IDENTITY TODAY

When the church adopted the term *Christian* from outsiders and began using it as a self-designation, it signified two things: They were willing to *stand up* for Christ and to *stand together* with one another. I hope this brief survey of the origins of the term will help sharpen the way you think of the word today. In some parts of the world, *Christian* carries nearly no religious connotation at all. It's simply a sociopolitical or ethnic designation for people who happen to be born not-Muslim, not-Hindu, and so on.

I do not know that I can change the way other people use (or misuse) the term *Christian*, but I hope I have influenced you. In fact, my aim has been to change the way you think about yourself and the Christians around you because the gospel has changed each of us individually and all of us together. We were not simply brought into a unique, reconciled relationship with God when we were saved. We were also brought into a unique relationship with one another because of our union with Jesus. Every term we have looked at preaches this message with its own distinct emphasis:

- *Brothers and sisters*: We choose solidarity because we belong to one another.
- *Beloved*: We begin with love, just as God did with us.
- *Saints*: We surround one another when the world goes dark.
- *Disciples*: We follow the Lord in a community of common surrender.
- *Fellow (fill-in-the-blank-with-a-noun-of-your-choice)-ers*: We suffer and strive together toward a common goal.
- *Christians*: We stand out because we stand together in Jesus' name.

Terms like these are not arbitrary labels. They are proclamations of the gospel, and each of us can proclaim this gospel! It may not feel natural at first, but it lies within everyone's reach. What we have in common because of Christ beggars whatever differences lie between us. We have been united to God in such a way that our personal preferences, tribal affiliations, and cultural distinctions are far less important than our identity as brothers and sisters, saints, and these other collective identities. Our differences don't get washed away in Christ, but they cease to circumscribe and separate us from the ones whom God loves.

When I think about the fierce loyalty many people show toward their political parties today, I wonder how such people, if they are Christians, can show fervent concern for policies and so little concern for their brothers and sisters. If we were half as invested in supporting the saints as we are in promoting the causes of politicians, the world might take notice. Human community that develops apart from the grace of God in Christ can only handle so much diversity without losing its way. The church can handle everyone whom God is pleased to save and set apart. Its diversity stretches as far as the Cross. In fact, from the inside, its people may not even seem that different since every face is the face of a family member. Inside the church, there is only family.

Each generation faces its unique social pressures, sinful impulses, and satanic deception. The church will always be in danger of internalizing the factionalism that defines relationships in the world. Cultural turf wars, class divisions, and tribal alliances tell us how we separate ourselves naturally. Only the church has a gospel strong enough to bring people together. In the New Testament, they called it a message of reconciliation. Believers preached this message using single, simple words when our faith was young. We can do so again. Call the Christian at your workplace your "brother" or "sister." Call the Christian who votes for the other party your "beloved brother [or sister]." Call your prayer group "God's people" (or "saints"). See what happens.

My friend Karen Stiller says it this way in her book *Holiness Here*: "We need to be told who we are out loud, right into our ears. And if this can happen in a church, all the better. . . . You are the beloved, go love. You are holy, go try to be even more fully that way. You might even enjoy yourself. The naming is a gift and a push. It says what is true now and points the way forward to what can more fully be."[1]

Instead of simply calling everyone around you a "Christian," call some of them "disciples" some of the time. Talk about how you are all "fellow partaker[s] in the tribulation and kingdom and perseverance which are in Jesus" (Revelation 1:9, one of my favorites). See what happens. People will notice, and you'll likely be a little uncomfortable. But don't stop speaking. The gospel doesn't change the world as we think about it. We have to open our mouths.

I hope you will not feel ashamed to proclaim this gospel in some of the ways I have outlined in this book. This was the language of the early church, after all—the language of the Scriptures themselves. Read your Bibles with greater attention to these words we so easily gloss over. Nurture these words of Christian self-designation in your mind. Then say it like it is, and see what happens.

# Acknowledgments

The concept for this book came from a single line in a research paper I had written for a class at Denver Seminary, a New Testament survey taught by Dr. Craig Blomberg. The paper had to do with Jesus' vision for discipleship. After I wrote it, I thought there might be something worth saying to a wider audience, so I sent the paper to Dave Zimmerman at NavPress. Out of the eighteen pages of stilted prose that comprised that paper, Dave picked out one sentence and said, "I don't think anyone has ever written a book on the fact that Christians didn't call themselves 'Christians' in the early days of the church. Would you be willing to follow up on that?" From that very brief comment, this absurdly long book has taken shape. Dave should be credited with the genesis of this book. He should not be blamed for any of its deficiencies.

I also owe a great debt of gratitude to another David. In the summer of 2022, I was stuck in the swamp of self-deprecation and low morale. I reached out to my friend David McGlynn, who is a teacher and author himself. I didn't deserve the amount of attention David gave me, but I think he realized that nothing good would come from abandoning me. So he stepped up to become something like a spiritual director, fellow sufferer, writing coach, and medieval executioner all-in-one. When I felt unable to sit and write another word, David was the grace of God toward me. When I did what he told me to do, it usually worked. When I stopped doing what he told me to do, he fined me ten dollars. Then he skipped my pity party. This book would never have been written without David's influence in my life. If you love the book, you can thank him. If you hate it, you could try asking him for that ten-dollar fine I paid.

I have benefited a great deal from the works of three New Testament scholars, and I should mention them here. Paul Trebilco has written a scholarly monograph entitled *Self-Designations and Group Identity in the New Testament*. It is the only work I have found that tackles a wide range of terms like the ones in this book, and it argues coherently for how these terms functioned in shaping Christian community in the first century. I am also indebted to Joseph Hellerman and his thorough study of the use, background, and influence of family language in the New Testament. His book on this is called *The Ancient Church as Family*. Finally, I have benefited immensely from Michael Wilkins's work entitled *Following the Master: A Biblical Theology of Discipleship*. I have spent so much time interacting with the work of these three scholars that their ideas have probably crept into this book in ways I cannot account for. I cite them when I know I am borrowing their words or ideas. I thank them here.

I suppose the list of people who have influenced this work could go on. Dr. Craig Blomberg at Denver Seminary and Dr. Michael Holmes, professor emeritus from Bethel University and Seminary, took the time to answer questions I threw at them via email in the early stages of my research. They owed me nothing, but they gave me much. They embody what it means to have the mind of a scholar and the heart of a teacher. My friend Nick Peterson offered helpful thoughts on several chapters. My daughter, Kayla Parker, and my sister-in-law, Erika Sterken, read the manuscript and offered sound advice for improving it.

Finally, I wish to say thank you to my wife, Kristy. She has uncanny intuition about what I need in the moment, whether it's a salad, a break, or a kick in the pants. We have walked through a great deal of loss over the years. Her faith in God, along with her love for me, makes the road ahead inviting, not forbidding.

# About the Author

**NORMAN HUBBARD** is the author of three Bible study guides: *Left of Matthew* (2007), *Right of Malachi* (2007), and *Calling God Names* (2013), all from NavPress. He graduated from Auburn University with a BA in literature and an MA in linguistics. Norman is currently completing an MDiv at Denver Seminary and serves the collegiate leadership team of The Navigators in resource and staff development. Norman and his wife, Kristy, live in Saint Paul, Minnesota.

# Notes

**INTRODUCTION | THE GOSPEL AND THE GAPS THAT SEPARATE US**

1. Miroslav Volf, professor of theology at Yale University, says it this way: "'Gospel' always involves a way of living in a given social environment as a Christian community. . . . To ask about how the gospel relates to culture is to ask how to live as a Christian *community* in a particular cultural context. . . . Indeed, there is no other way to reflect adequately on gospel and culture except by reflecting on how the social embodiments of the gospel relate to a given culture." Miroslav Volf, "Soft Difference: Theological Reflections on the Relation between Church and Culture in 1 Peter," *Ex Auditu* 10 (1994): 16.

2. "The association of this title ['Christian'] with such sobriquets as 'murderer' and 'thief' can be construed to mean our author here refers to penalties imposed on Christians by courts of law simply because they were Christians." Paul J. Achtemeier, *1 Peter: A Commentary on First Peter*, ed. Eldon Jay Epp, Hermeneia—a Critical and Historical Commentary on the Bible (Minneapolis: Fortress Press, 1996), 313.

3. See, for example, St Andrews Encyclopaedia of Theology on "Baptism in the History of Religion," https://www.saet.ac.uk/Christianity/Baptism #section2.

4. Rodney Stark, *The Rise of Christianity: How the Obscure, Marginal Jesus Movement Became the Dominant Religious Force in the Western World in a Few Centuries* (San Francisco: HarperSanFrancisco, 1997), 208. Stark is a sociologist at the University of Washington who studies religious movements. Here is the context of his comment: "Christianity *did not* grow because of miracle working in the marketplaces . . . or because

Constantine said it should, or even because the martyrs gave it such credibility. It grew because Christians constituted an intense community. . . . And the primary means of its growth was through the united and motivated efforts of the growing numbers of Christian believers, who invited their friends, relatives, and neighbors to share the 'good news.'"

5. John M. G. Barclay, *Pauline Churches and Diaspora Jews* (Grand Rapids: Eerdmans, 2016), 101.

6. "Ananias addressed him as 'Brother Saul' or 'Saul, my brother' (NEB). I never fail to be moved by these words. They may well have been the first words which Saul heard from Christian lips after his conversion, and they were words of fraternal welcome. They must have been music to his ears. What? Was the arch-enemy of the church to be welcomed as a brother? Was the dreaded fanatic to be received as a member of the family? Yes, it was so." John R. W. Stott, *The Message of Acts*, The Bible Speaks Today (Downers Grove, IL: InterVarsity Press, 1990), 175–76.

7. Paul Trebilco, *Self-Designations and Group Identity in the New Testament* (Cambridge, UK: Cambridge University Press, 2012), chap. 1.

8. Trebilco, *Self-Designations*, chap. 1.

### CHAPTER 1 | THE POWER OF GOD AND THE POWER OF WORDS

1. *Woman* (Hebrew *'iššâ*, pronounced *ish-shaw'*) is the same word as *man* (Hebrew *'îš*, pronounced *eesh*), but with the feminine ending. I believe this indicates that the woman is like in kind to the man as a human, though different in gender.

2. I have felt some tension writing this sentence (and this book) and referring to "Christians" in the early days of "Christianity." Those were not terms the early church used to describe themselves. However, it seemed cumbersome or contrived to use other terms, given how accustomed we are to the word *Christian*. For the sake of readability, I have opted to own the awkwardness of using the word *Christian* (a lot) while making my argument that the early church used a richer vocabulary of self-designation.

3. Actually, this *is* a linguistic theory known as speech act theory. However, as good linguistic theories should, this one describes in technical language something we all experience in common life.

### CHAPTER 2 | THE FULL FORCE OF THE GOSPEL

1. G. K. Chesterton, *The Everlasting Man* (London: Hodder and Stoughton, 1926), 13.

2. "The gospel is the announcement that God's kingdom has come in the life, death, and resurrection of Jesus of Nazareth, the Lord and Messiah, in

fulfillment of Israel's Scriptures. The gospel evokes faith, repentance, and discipleship; its accompanying effects include salvation and the gift of the Holy Spirit." Michael F. Bird, *Evangelical Theology: A Biblical and Systematic Introduction*, 2nd ed. (Grand Rapids: Zondervan, 2020), 37.

3. Though I am not prepared to argue the point here, sanctification should probably be regarded as a fourth force of the gospel. The New Testament presents it not only as the ongoing work of Christians but also as the finished work of Christ (see, for example, 1 Corinthians 1:2, 30; 6:11; Hebrews 10:10).

4. I capitalize Sin and Death in this list because they are sometimes portrayed as personified cosmic powers in the New Testament. They are not regarded as abstract concepts or theological consequences of the Fall. Rather, they are regarded as enemies of humanity and usurpers of authority.

5. The verbs *united* and *freed* draw attention to themselves in this passage because they appear in the relatively rare perfect tense in Greek.

## CHAPTER 3 | THE REALITY OF RECONCILIATION

1. Jerry Bridges, *Trusting God: Even When Life Hurts* (Colorado Springs: NavPress, 2008), 139–40.

2. Rodney Stark, *The Rise of Christianity: How the Obscure, Marginal Jesus Movement Became the Dominant Religious Force in the Western World in a Few Centuries* (San Francisco: HarperSanFrancisco, 1997), 157–58.

3. Stark, *Rise of Christianity*, 160–61.

4. John M. G. Barclay, *Pauline Churches and Diaspora Jews* (Grand Rapids: Eerdmans, 2016), 79.

## CHAPTER 4 | BROTHERS AND SISTERS IN THE TIME OF THE NEW TESTAMENT

1. In chapter 3, we learned that a *register* is a patterned way of speaking to signal closeness or distance in a social setting.

2. Throughout this book, I will refer to the way Christians talked *to* and *about* one another as "self-designation." This is the term used by New Testament scholar Paul Trebilco in his monograph *Self-Designations and Group Identity in the New Testament*.

3. I can't remember how old I was—probably a young teenager—when I learned that Cowboy was his nickname. His actual name was Calvin, but I never heard anyone call him by that name. Perhaps because he was a Baptist.

4. The Greek term translated as "brothers" or "brothers and sisters" is *adelphoi*. The context of a passage usually makes clear whether the author means "brothers" (i.e., "male brothers") or "brothers and sisters" (i.e., "siblings"). A close parallel in modern English involves our use of the

word *guys*. This word can be used to refer to men only (e.g., the "guys' restroom" instead of the "girls' restroom"). However, it is often used in mixed-gender settings to refer to men and women (e.g., "Would you guys stop talking and listen to me?") In Greek, all nouns and adjectives have a grammatical gender: masculine, feminine, or neuter. Though the grammatical gender sometimes reflects the sexual gender of the object referred to, that's not always the case. For instance, the word *brotherhood* in Greek (*adelphotēs*) is a grammatically feminine noun.

5. See, for instance, Jesus' question in Matthew 5:47: "If you greet only your brothers, what more are you doing than others? Do not even the Gentiles do the same?" Or Peter's calling the "men of Judea and all you who live in Jerusalem" "Brethren" (Acts 2:14, 29).

6. Joseph H. Hellerman, *The Ancient Church as Family* (Minneapolis: Fortress Press, 2001).

7. "As important as mother-son relationships are to the PKG [patrilineal kinship group] family matrix, it is yet another relational bond that truly defines what it means to be a part of a patrilineal family group. At the very heart of the PKG ideal is the sibling solidarity so characteristic of Mediterranean families. Indeed, sibling relationships reflect perhaps the most important distinction between ancient PKGs and modern Western kindred systems. And it is the PKG sibling relational model that the followers of Jesus appropriate in their image of the church as family." Hellerman, *Ancient Church as Family*, 35.

8. The grace of God in the Old Testament truly stands out against the backdrop of broken solidarity in Israel's founding families. Esau wanted to murder Jacob. Joseph's brothers sold him into slavery in Egypt after contemplating killing him. Stories like these magnify the mercy of God and his fidelity to his promises.

## CHAPTER 5 | THE GOSPEL OF RECONCILIATION IN ONE WORD

1. It would be fascinating for someone to find the first clear use of "Brother" as a title within the church. I speculate it happened during the first monastic period, several hundred years after the close of the New Testament; however, my limited resources have not permitted me to explore this question.

2. "Martyrdom of Polycarp," in *The Apostolic Fathers in English*, rev. Michael W. Holmes (Grand Rapids: Baker Academic, 2006), 154.

3. How did Philemon respond? We don't know, but we can assume things turned out favorably. First, the letter Paul wrote to Philemon was

preserved and passed down as Holy Scripture. That would hardly have happened if Philemon had thrown it in the garbage and ignored Paul's counsel. Second, there's a tantalizing detail from Ignatius's letter to the Ephesians (written in the early 100s): The author mentions a church leader by the name of Onesimus (Ignatius, "To the Ephesians," in *The Apostolic Fathers in English*, 97). The name was common enough for slaves in the Roman Empire, so there's no way to guarantee that this is the same Onesimus, but the speculation seems sound. Ephesus wasn't that far from Colossae after all.

4. Name has been changed.

5. Eugene Terekhin has recently chronicled this family's flight from Russia in the self-published book *The New Exodus: Escaping One Man's War*. You can find a copy here: https://store.restandtrust.org /products/the-new-exodus-escaping-putins-war-1.

## CHAPTER 6 | BELOVED

1. "We may therefore safely take it that the letter is being written by Paul, in prison . . . to Philemon, who lived, and had the oversight of a house-church, in Colosse. Tychicus and Onesimus are taking with them not only the main Colossian letter (Col. 4:7-9) but also this more personal note to one of the church's leaders." N. T. Wright, *The Epistles of Paul to the Colossians and to Philemon: An Introduction and Commentary* (Grand Rapids: Eerdmans, 1986), 165–66.

2. "Because ἀγαπητῷ is followed by the coordinative καί, it is not an adj[ective] qualifying συνεργῷ. With the art[icle] (τῷ) the adj[ective] ἀγαπητός is a subst[antive] . . ." Murray J. Harris, *Colossians and Philemon* (Nashville: B&H Academic, 2010), 211.

3. Because I introduced you to my late wife, Katie, earlier in this book, I should probably mention that I am remarried to Kristy.

4. Paul Trebilco refers to this as the "horizontal axis" of self-designation in the New Testament. Some terms tell us about our identify before God (the vertical axis), while others, like *beloved*, tell us about our relationship to one another in Christ (the horizontal axis). See Paul Trebilco, *Self-Designations and Group Identity in the New Testament* (UK: Cambridge University Press, 2012), 303.

5. E.g., 1 John 4:11. This is not a modern phenomenon. Even Wycliffe translated "beloved" from the Latin *carissimi* as "moost dere britheren" or "most dear brothers."

6. Prince grew up going to Park Avenue Methodist in downtown Minneapolis.

He probably heard "dearly beloved" in church a time or two as a kid before recording "Let's Go Crazy" as an adult. He certainly heard it when he and his first wife were married at Park Avenue Methodist. (See https://www .minnesotaumc.org/newsdetail/park-avenue-umc-was-part-of-princes-life -faith-journey-4595697.)

7. "Its paucity in gener[al] Gk. lit. may be due to a presumed colloq[ial] flavor of the noun . . ." Frederick William Danker, ed., *A Greek-English Lexicon of the New Testament and Other Early Christian Literature*, 3rd ed., based on Walter Bauer's *Griechish-deutsches Wörterbuch zu den Schriften des Neuen Testaments und der frühchristlichen Literatur*, 6th ed. (Chicago: University of Chicago Press, 2000), 6.

8. Ceslaus Spicq, *Agape in the New Testament*, vol. 1: *Agape in the Synoptic Gospels*, trans. Marie Aquinas McNamara and Mary Honoria Richter (Eugene, OR: Wipf & Stock, 2006), 12.

## CHAPTER 7 | SAINTS

1. *Merriam-Webster*, s.v. "saint (*n.*)," accessed February 20, 2024, https:// www.merriam-webster.com/dictionary/saint.

2. I make myself responsible for any error in the count here. Because the Greek *hagios* can be used as an attributive or substantive adjective, sometimes a judgment call has to be made about how it is being used in a given context. There are also instances (e.g., Revelation 22:11) where *hagios* is used in the singular, but it seems to refer to a class or kind of people.

3. The dominant sense of the word is "being dedicated or consecrated to the service of God . . . reserved for God and God's service." Frederick William Danker, ed., *A Greek-English Lexicon of the New Testament and Other Early Christian Literature*, 3rd ed., based on Walter Bauer's *Griechisch-deutsches Wörterbuch zu den Schriften des Neuen Testaments und der frühchristlichen Literatur*, 6th ed. (Chicago: University of Chicago Press, 2000), 10. Harold Hoehner also helpfully says, "When the term [*saints*] is used to refer to things, places, and persons, it does not in itself connote any inherent holiness. . . . The basic idea is that which is consecrated to God or to God's service." Harold W. Hoehner, *Ephesians: An Exegetical Commentary* (Grand Rapids: Baker Academic, 2002), 138.

4. The election of Israel as God's chosen people is handled somewhat differently in rabbinic thought. An overview of rabbinic perspectives can be found in Abraham Cohen, *Everyman's Talmud: The Major Teachings of the Rabbinic Sages*, repr. (New York: Schocken Books, 1995), 60–62.

5. Taken from a chart in Craig Blomberg and Darlene Seal's *From Pentecost to Patmos*. The authors argue that many of the sins mentioned in the

Corinthian correspondence stem from the misuse of wealth and power in that church. See Craig L. Blomberg and Darlene M. Seal with Alicia S. Duprée, *From Pentecost to Patmos: An Introduction to Acts through Revelation*, 2nd ed. (Nashville: B&H Academic, 2021), 243.

6. I am ready to make the concession that *saints* has been so misrepresented from medieval to modern times that we need an alternative to it. I have begun saying something like "We are the people of God" or "Since God has set us apart together for his purposes . . ." These phrases are a little less elegant than *saints*, but they seem less likely to connote moral exceptionalism.

## CHAPTER 8 | DISCIPLES

1. Mandy Patinkin as Inigo Montoya in *The Princess Bride* (Los Angeles: Twentieth Century Fox, 1987).

2. In his list of "common fallacies in semantics," D. A. Carson lists "the root fallacy" first. The root fallacy "presupposes that every word actually *has* a meaning bound up with its shape or its components. . . . All of this is linguistic nonsense." D. A. Carson, *Exegetical Fallacies*, 2nd ed. (Grand Rapids: Baker Academic, 1996), 26, 39.

3. Michael Wilkins, a New Testament scholar from Talbot School of Theology, says, "We have strong evidence that believers, most of whom would never have had any contact with Jesus in his earthly ministry, continued to identify themselves as Jesus' disciples long after he had ascended. Further, one of the most prominent terms for Christians in the writings of Ignatius, the overseer of the church at Antioch, is *disciple*, indicating that believers continued to identify themselves as Jesus' followers into the second century." Michael J. Wilkins, *Following the Master: Discipleship in the Steps of Jesus* (Grand Rapids: Zondervan, 1992), 286.

4. DesiringGod.org, "What Is Discipleship and How Is It Done?" January 25, 2016, in *Ask Pastor John* (podcast), episode 779, https://www.desiringgod.org/interviews/what-is-discipleship-and-how-is-it-done.

## CHAPTER 9 | FELLOW WORKERS

1. Since English borrows heavily from Greek, we see the direct influence of the prefix *syn-* in words like *synthesis, sympathy, symmetrical,* and *synagogue* (an assembly that gathers together).

2. The list provided here is not exhaustive but representative of the number of times terms like these are used outside the Gospels and Acts as terms of self-designation among believers. In the original Greek, these words are

as follows. Fellow worker: *synergos*; fellow prisoner: *synaichmalōtos*; fellow partaker: *sygkoinōnos*; fellow slave: *syndoulos*; fellow soldier: *systratiōtēs*; fellow citizen: *sympolitēs*; fellow member: *syssōmos*; fellow sharer: *symmetochos*; fellow member of the elect: *syneklektos*.

3. Because this form of self-designation has not been studied in the academic literature, I cannot say whether the *syn-* combinations found in the New Testament were common in the wider Greco-Roman world. My hunch is that the Christian community used these words in new or unusual ways. For instance, I bet that members of a craftsmen's guild referred to one another as "fellow workers." But they would not use this term for people who didn't practice their trade. Christians were using this term in an altogether strange way.

4. Joseph H. Hellerman, *Philippians*, Exegetical Guide to the Greek New Testament, ed. Andreas J. Köstenberger and Robert W. Yarbrough (Nashville: B&H Academic, 2015), 156.

5. Colin G. Kruse, *The Second Epistle of Paul to the Corinthians: An Introduction and Commentary*, Tyndale New Testament Commentaries (Grand Rapids: Eerdmans, 1987), 78.

6. For more information about this giant boot, see https://www.loc.gov/item /2020723684.

## CHAPTER 10 | CHRISTIANS

1. "While the occurrence of the term in Acts 11:26 indicates, at the very least, the recognition by Gentiles that believers in Christ were an entity separate from both pagan Gentiles and Judaism, the other two occurrences in the NT [New Testament] possibly indicate that elements of *contempt* (Acts 26:28) and *hostility* (1 Pet 4:16) were attached to the term by the early use of those outside of the church. There is no NT evidence that the term was commonly used as a self-designation by the early church." Michael J. Wilkins, "Christian," in *The Anchor Bible Dictionary*, Vol. 1: A–C, ed. David Noel Freedman (New York: Doubleday, 1992), 926. Emphasis added.

2. "Ignatius to the Romans, Letter III," in *The Apostolic Fathers*, vol. 1, trans. Kirsopp Lake, The Loeb Classical Library (New York: MacMillan, 1912), 229. Emphasis added.

3. "The Martyrdom of Polycarp" 9:3–10:1, in *The Apostolic Fathers: Greek Texts and English Translations*, 3rd ed., trans. and ed. Michael W. Holmes, after the earlier work of J. B. Lightfoot and J. R. Harmer (Grand Rapids: Baker Academic, 2007), 317. Emphasis added.

4. "The Martyrdom of Polycarp" 12.1–12.3, in *The Apostolic Fathers*, trans. and ed. Michael W. Holmes, 319.
5. "The Epistle to Diognetus" 1:1, in *The Apostolic Fathers*, trans. and ed. Michael W. Holmes, 695. Emphasis added.
6. "The Epistle to Diognetus" 5:1–5, in *The Apostolic Fathers*, trans. and ed. Michael W. Holmes, 701–3. Emphasis added.
7. Sozomenus, "The Ecclesiastical History of Sozomen," in *A Select Library of Nicene and Post-Nicene Fathers of the Christian Church*, ed. Philip Schaff and Henry Wace, trans. Chester D. Hartranft, vol. 2, *Socrates, Sozomenus: Church Histories* (New York: Christian Literature Co., 1890), 338. Emphasis added.

## EPILOGUE | THE LANGUAGE OF CHRISTIAN IDENTITY TODAY

1. Karen Stiller, *Holiness Here: Searching for God in the Ordinary Events of Everyday Life* (Colorado Springs: NavPress, 2024), 26.

## NavPress is the book-publishing arm of The Navigators.

Since 1933, The Navigators has helped people around the world bring hope and purpose to others in college campuses, local churches, workplaces, neighborhoods, and hard-to-reach places all over the world, face-to-face and person-by-person in an approach we call Life-to-Life® discipleship. We have committed together to know Christ, make Him known, and help others do the same.®

Would you like to join this adventure of discipleship and disciplemaking?

- Take a Digital Discipleship Journey at **navigators.org/disciplemaking**.
- Get more discipleship and disciplemaking content at **thedisciplemaker.org**.
- Find your next book, Bible, or discipleship resource at **navpress.com**.

 @NavPressPublishing

 @NavPress

 @navpressbooks

CP1790